A Rhyme for Everything

Rhythmic Poetry for Everyone

Kathleen J. Shields

ISBN: 978-1-941345-44-3   Paperback

ISBN-E: 9780463221969   Smashwords

ASIN-E: B07ZHM57FY   Kindle

ERIN GO BRAGH
Publishing

Canyon Lake, TX

www.ErinGoBraghPublishing.com

Table of Contents

STORY TIME Poems

INSPIRATIONAL Poems

CHALLENGE & CHANGE Poems

MUSICAL Poems

FAMILY & FRIENDS Poems

Introduction

When I was a child my favorite author was Dr. Seuss care of all of those fun rhythmic rhymes he used in his stories. Of course as an adult I found his use of imaginary words and phrases a let-down. To me, it almost seemed like cheating. Yes rhyming can be difficult, but when I rhyme in my children's books, if I use a word that a child may not know, I'll define it on the page to increase vocabulary. But that's beside the point.

My next favorite book was 'Twas the Night Before Christmas, and THAT book changed my life. I went from Roses are Red poems to 'Twas the day before middle school" in a snap of a finger.

I had "The Real Mother Goose" an assortment of poems that would make you cringe if you really thought about their subject and contents. "Where the Sidewalk Ends" and "The Missing Piece meets the Big O" which of course the latter didn't rhyme but it always made me think. And of course, "The Little Engine That Could", which gave me the inspiration to know that I could do anything, if put my mind to it – and I did.

Giving credit to my favorite rhyming books, my poems got longer. I started carrying around a rhyming dictionary. I started thinking about words alphabetically. If I started with cat, I'd find rhymes in alphabetical order: at, bat, fat, hat, (g)nat, mat, pat, rat, sat.... I began learning two-syllable words: bobcat, combat, doormat...

By the time I got to high school I was thinking Rhyme – All of the time!

It started a game with friends and fellow students. With eight minutes between class to get to your locker and 'socialize' I announced a challenge. I was given a topic and one minute; timed. And with that – I would write at least a two stanza poem to wow the crowd. The poem may not have been anything life changing, but it was enough to make them laugh in astonishment.

"Come up with a poem about pizza." They knew the word pizza, like purple and orange don't have any real rhymes. They thought they'd stump me.

"Okay..." I'd say, and in less than one minute later I presented the following poem:

> I like pizza, yes I do, I like pizza, why don't you?
> I like pizza with lots of meat,
> I think pizza's really neat.

Before long I was writing poetry for greeting cards, cards that needed some sort of graphic with it, so I began sourcing images, mixing in words and graphics – little did I know, that began my love and future career of graphic design.

One of my most popular poems is "Angels are Mothers" which has made its way around the country via social media every Mother's Day for decades. That poem has been published in magazines and newspapers. It all started as a Mother's Day poem I wrote, printed on a rainbow background and framed for my mom almost thirty years ago.

Rhyming created "The Hamilton Troll Adventures" my educational children's book series. It all started with a poem about a troll who met a fairy in 1992. A decade later, an illustrator drew Hamilton and now it's twelve story books strong with a coloring book, curriculum workbook and even a children's cookbook, with, you guessed it, a short rhyming story with each recipe!

My rhymes have even found their way into music, not professionally – yet, but I've written my own lyrics to some of my favorite songs. I did it quite a while ago. I even sang those songs and produced my own videos to go along with them. I am not proud of what I produced, I am not a professional singer, my videos were in the learning process and the music was from midis – however, the one I wrote those songs for, Smurpy the Wonder Dog, well he thoroughly enjoyed them.

It's always been a dream to brainstorm lyrics with a musician or two, heck, it's a dream to talk with every musician out there who chooses to use cusswords in songs, rather than finding a way to make their music family friendly. I realize they do it for ratings, for street cred, but it's not cool, in my opinion. When you hear a song on the radio and they bleep out words or silence it for a second, to me it's profound. Why would you want your work edited like that? Why would you want to put anything out there that a parent has to shield their child from, or that you can't play for your own grandmother? Just saying...

So needless to say, my poems are clean. Some of the ones in here were written in some dark times, but they were written to help me work through things. When I am feeling emotional, my mind turns to rhyme. Sadness, loneliness, grief, they draw the poetic out of me, but so does happiness, inspiration and joy.

Some of the poems are from high school.
Some were written during down days.
Some were written just for fun,
and some were written to express praise.
Yet no matter the poem, situation or time,
the point of my poems is that they rhyme!

I hope you enjoy my poetry. I would love to hear from you if you have something touch you profoundly. If you ever want to share one of my poems with a friend or family member, you are welcome to – so long as my name is attached.

Poetry is meant to be shared and enjoyed.
Please do so.

Ecclesiastes 3

I have always loved this scripture, along with the corresponding song "Turn! Turn! Turn!" by The Byrds as this was one my mother would play on her record player late at night to reminisce of better times.

This is why and how I chose the title of my book – as a play on words with Rhyme instead of Time and that the book kind of covers everything, from happiness to sadness, from life to death, from family to friends, following my dreams, being crazy and just saying thanks. An excerpt of the scripture is as follows:

> *There is a time for everything, and a season for every activity under the heavens: a time to be born and a time to die, a time to plant and a time to uproot, a time to kill and a time to heal, a time to tear down and a time to build, a time to weep and a time to laugh, a time to mourn and a time to dance, a time to search and a time to give up, a time to keep and a time to throw away, a time to tear and a time to mend, a time to be silent and a time to speak, a time to love and a time to hate, a time for war and a time for peace. (NIV)*
>
> ***I pray you find a rhyme to inspire you.***

BEING AN AUTHOR
Poems

100 Pages Till I Sleep

It's early Monday morning
And I'm up before the dawn,

A story on my mind,
Gotta type but then I yawn.

Coffee percolating,
Sleep wiped from my eyes,

I settle down to start before
The neighbors rooster cries.

I'll listen to the story
Playing loudly in my head,

And transcribe each scene,
Exactly as they said.

I'll write the heroes' messages,
Every whisper, scream and peep.

Until the story's finished,
A hundred pages 'till I sleep.

An Author's Mind

Unicorns and Aliens
Exist within this land.
Underwater mermaids,
An army takes a stand.

Dragon's soar the sky
with witches on their brooms,
Golden ticket doors
And secret magic rooms.

A world of vibrant rainbows
Written in a book
Chapters of Adventures
Readers take a look!

The eye of the beholder
Nothing as it seems...
An author lives a life
No others dare to dream.

Once Upon a Time

Once upon a time, an idea came to me,
I decided that I'd try to fly and leapt out of a tree.

Once upon a time, I knew I'd be a star
I sang within my bedroom walls,
But never ventured far.

Once upon a time, I fell for love so strong
But I was young, and I grew up,
it didn't last that long.

Once upon a time, I chose to write a book,
Looking back a decade plus, what a step I took.

I may not truly fly, but in my dreams I soar
I write about the fun my characters have in store.

Hollywood doesn't know me, but that's not my loss
At least I hold my head up,
With strength to bear my cross.

My love is my adventure, I share with others, too
Struggled life's experiences, help me do what I do.

At least my effort's fruitful,
I've never bowed to doubt
Because "Once upon a time", is what it's all about.

I know if I keep at it, my dreams will never fail
Cuz doubt kills more dreams than failure ever will.

Imagination

I hope by now you realize,
My brain is my best friend,
It helps me every day
Understand and comprehend.

It keeps me moving forward,
It warns me to go back,
It heightens my adrenaline,
When I'm on the attack.

My brain keeps me breathing,
My blood keeps on the flow,
My brain regulates everything,
It keeps me on the go.

But most of all my brain
Provides imagination,
It dreams about the craziest,
Worlds of its creation.

It takes me on adventures
While staying safe at home.
Exploring any place,
That my mind chooses to roam.

Imagination takes you
To dangers, fun and places,
So you can all appreciate,
Such fascinating faces!

Inspiring Youth

My motto is:

The only limitation is your own imagination...

Not only does it say exactly what I am trying to teach,
it also rhymes. How great is that?

> So when I'm talking to children,
> At shows or at their school,
> I'll explain how writing's awesome,
> And imagination's cool.
>
> I'll help then think out of the box,
> I'll help their minds have fun,
> I'll help them tell a story,
> Writing's for everyone!
>
> And fiction's even better,
> You don't have to tell the truth.
> A story is just telling,
> That's how I inspire youth.

Writing

My world is an adventure,
The weather changes fast.
Lightning turns to Sunshine,
The future turns to past.

Writing is but words,
Deciding how they'll fall.
I'm a God upon my planet,
And I dictate to them all.

My characters like humans,
They choose whom they will be.
They tell me of their plans,
I simply write to see.

Since I'm the final edit,
I can change their life quite quick,
And seeing how they'll turn out,
Is a rewarding writers trick.

Creation

Creation is key straight from conception
And with me there's never an exception.

Uniquely constructed,
My designs hold true
I'm proud when they make
Their initial debut.

But no story will end,
No picture complete
A life just goes on,
There's never defeat.

Originality continues,
Creativity lingers
As new ideas spill
Through my fingers.

Thoughts in Rhyme

My mind is kind of crazy,
When I start to think in rhyme,
There's a rhythm and a bounce,
Every line in perfect time.

Any subject, or event,
Every pulsating heartbeat,
It's a poet's life in verse,
Every moment is a treat.

When the rhyming stops,
I finally get rest.
But I know that it'll be hard,
I won't be at my best.

As my poetry must flow,
Like the Nile's rushing stream,
Always dreaming thoughts in tune,
Rhyming poetry extreme.

Rainbows in My Mind

The colors are amazing, an array to mystify,
Every color of the rainbow, present in the sky.

They tend to drift my way, and to my twinkling eyes,
Through my imagination, where it instigates surprise.

Within my mind are miracles, anything can happen,
Sliding on a rainbow, let's open up the wrappin'.

Every aspect that they touch, makes life a lil bit better
Every problem that I had, becomes a good forgetter.

Every person that I see, has potential to be great,
No circumstance holds back, you'll never be too late,

To become what God wants of you,
You seek and ye shall find
All the colors of the spectrum,
In the rainbows of my mind.

Never Second Guess Yourself

I was told the other day,
My thinking was unique,
I was way too young to them,
For this rare critique.

First impressions are important,
Listen to instinct,
But most of the time you don't,
You second guess what you think.

Have you ever done that,
Looked back and said "Oh,
Should have done this differently,"
Like you missed the memo?

Well I've done that so much,
In my rather special life,
I've decided to now listen,
To avoid that undo strife.

Next time an opportunity,
Is presented and I feel
The need to second guess myself,
To haggle, shake or deal,

I'll go with my first instinct,
That feeling, sense or hunch,
It's there 'cuz it's important,
It's a spiritual fist punch.

No matter what you call it -
Women's intuition?
It's anything but odd,
It's like a premonition.

Your feelings 'bout a person
Usually are right.
The decision you should make,
Consider your first sight.

With time comes proclivity,
Your gut dictates your knack,
Your experiences in life
Keep you right on track.

So listen to your impulse,
Go ahead and get that cake,
Never second guess yourself,
Your life is what YOU make.

If I were...

If I were a unicorn
I would have caught the ark,
So I'd still be around today
To leave my magic mark.

If I were a dinosaur,
I'd might have said a prayer,
In hopes that the asteroid
Wouldn't land, you know where.

If I were a Dodo,
I should have learned to fly.
Just because you fail one time,
Doesn't mean you shouldn't try.

If I were a dragon,
I'd protect the good from evil.
It's a shame we didn't learn
From the ancient times, medieval.

If I were a wooly mammoth,
I would have fought them back,
I wonder what would have been,
If I'd won the attack?

If I were a mermaid,
I think I'd rather be,
Swimming in the ocean,
Instead of being me.

But no matter what I'd do,
There'd always be some sad,
Because apparently you can't have good
Without a little bad.

The dark is not the point,
The change comes with the light,
Whatever's in your past,
It's there, wrong or right.

It's an aspect of the world,
You're here and then you're gone.
Our stories are the race,
And each telling's the baton.

I wish...

I wish I'd meet somebody,
Who read my book and then
Would tell me how they loved it,
And then buy from me again.

I wish my book would make it,
Into the hands of a
Producer for a TV show, yeah,
That would be the day.

I wish that I could see my words
Up on the giant screen,
Enjoyed by countless others,
That is quite a dream.

I wish the sales were plentiful,
At least to pay the bills,
I wish my books did more for folks,
So they would share my thrills.

But a wish is not a plan for life,
A wish is all downhill
Stop saying that I wish,
And start saying that I will.

I will keep writing fiction,
I will keep writing tales,
I will keep publishing books,
And I will keep getting sales.

I will keep working at it,
Until I breathe no more,
Because I will keep trying,
To open up those doors.

And if they never open,
At least I'll know I tried,
Working towards my wishes,
Until the day I died.

Who knows what the future's planning,
I'll never just be still,
Because I'm not just wishing,
It's engraved within my will.

When Writing Calls

If you ever see me writing, frantically insane,
Give me just a moment, because I am in pain.

I'm aching to get the idea, out from my head,
Burning to get it written, before the flames spread.

My muscles may be cramping, but I must write on,
My imagination forces me, I am just its pawn.

Discomfort that I'm feeling, is just a fading crick,
'Cause when the idea's written, I know it'll be slick.

No wounds or affliction will give a twinge of doubt,
And if you try to interrupt, I just may have to shout.

Stories are like good soufflé, they so easily can fall,
No matter what they won't come back, even if I call.

Then the mental suffering, the anguish and the grief
Will torment those characters, until there is relief.

So if you see me writing, appreciate my walls,
That tribulation happens, only when writing calls.

I'm an Open Book

Ask me a question, but be prepared,
You will get the truth, as if you cared.

If you ask how I'm feeling, honesty is mine,
You won't get generic, if I am not fine.

I'll tell you the truth because that's how I like it,
I hope that's okay, some don't, I'll admit.

I was always taught to give what I want to receive,
I will always want the truth, please don't deceive.

Because I will believe you, but never again,
You lie to me, that is the end.

Ask me a question, and be on the hook,
I'll tell you right now, I'm an open book.

Where Have All The Good Rhymes Gone?

Confused about poems, I'll not deny,
If I can't rhyme, I'd rather cry.
But true that there are a bunch of choices,
For those with alternating voices.

A sonnet in iambic pentameter,
Is definitely not for the poetry cheater
A seventeen syllable haiku,
Is something most can get through.

Elegy for mourning, epitaph for graves,
But why stop there, let's make some waves.
A cleverly short epigram,
I'll take that if on the exam.

A limerick is quick and it is funny,
But not as easy, if I'm betting money.
Many ballads are long just like odes,
To tell a story long as roads.

Free verse feels not free to me,
You can do what you want, it's anarchy!
At least an epitaph can rhyme,
And sonnets tend to, I won't deny.

Needless to say, I could feel withdrawn,
As I wonder where have all the good rhymes gone?

Wasting My Rhyme

There's been many times, throughout my life,
I've wasted a good rhyme.

So many times they start off great,
The rhythm and the time.

But then they peter out half-way,
And I can't find the moral,

I try to work the story out,
But it builds an inner quarrel.

I erase the last two stanzas,
Move the others towards the end,

But no matter how I write them,
I can't play or pretend,

Some poems find their way to me,
Some poems they do not,

And so those wonderful beginnings
Are just wasted after thought.

RHYME AFTER TIME
Poems

A Matter of Rhyme

The world keeps on spinning, so what does it matter
If people say things in their daily chatter?

It's a matter of priorities, where do they fall?
Are those the people, with whom you'd call?

No matter how small their words make you feel,
It's up to you to take time to heal.

It's a matter of time, it's a matter of faith,
It's a choice to love or a decision to hate.

As a matter of fact, it's mind over matter,
If you don't mind, it doesn't matter.

Because you matter to me, all of you reading,
To those that are not, I know that you're needing.

You may feel unworthy, or think you are flawed.
But every one of us is a child of God.

Remember you're loved, somebody out there,
They may not say it, but they do care.

And if you're somebody who falls to the latter,
Make sure the other, knows they matter.

Rhyme Waits For No One

The clock hands are spinning, around they go,
Spinning faster and faster like a tornado.

They never stop, or get applause,
Time never waits, it'll never pause.

Just keep ticking, there goes the time,
A constant countdown, an uphill climb.

The direction you take, it may look strange,
But if it is called for, it's time for change.

You don't have all the time in the world,
Time pulls apart and gets unfurled.

It's not just on clocks, just watch the sun,
Time always flies when you're having fun.

Timing is everything, don't wait till it's right,
Keep moving forward with every green light.

What time is it? It's time for fun,
Enjoy this life, it waits for no one.

Adventure Rhyme

It's time for an adventure, into the unknown,
You can bring all your friends or take it alone.

You can soar in the sky or the depths of the sea,
All you need is the desire to be carefree.

Dream you are awesome, with powers galore,
You never know what you have in store.

Adventure is key to imagine the great,
Worlds full of fun to captivate.

Be brave, read a book, and lift yourself higher,
Live an adventure, anything you desire.

Daylight Savings Rhyme

First spring forward and then fall back,
My yearly schedule is on attack,

I remember not knowing which to do,
I truly didn't have a single clue.

When I was a child all I was told,
Is come in before dark, sunset threshold.

Remember the summers, those evenings were long,
But then in the winter, now that was wrong.

Hours before bedtime, it began to get dark,
I couldn't go play out in the park.

Granted it was getting cold, didn't want to be out,
But my playtime was cut and that made me pout.

Now that's I'm older, it cuts into my sleep,
An hour to me, well, that's mine to keep.

Can't get stuff done, when it's cool enough to do it,
When the daylight is right, it's too hot, I'll admit.

Maybe, just maybe, the savings are useless,
To fall back my time is actually fruitless.

I'm sure there's a reason for this annual assault,
We call it Daylight Savings, and it is at fault.

Don't Waste My Rhyme

If I'm writing a poem, and my first line ends with at,
Don't just think my rhyming, will end the next with cat.

Yes, that may be easy, and yes, I've done it personally,
Rhyming poems carefully, can't be written forcefully.

Poems have no end in sight, no set beginning either,
Words pronounced in other ways,
Get thrown into the fryer -
(unless you pronounced either with something that
sounds like a non-believer.)

Poems also take hold of their story,
If you can't find a rhyme,
You go to the thesaurus,
And change the word each time.
And if you can't find a word
That instills the message desired,
You get rid of the line altogether,
That idea's fired.

Many times you'll discover, the poem's finally finished,
It turns out much better, than you had ever wished.

Poetry takes practice, and patience over time,
Simply don't assume, & please don't waste my rhyme.

Rhyme of My Life

One of my favorite movies of all time,
Had not one word of poetic rhyme.

Instead it dealt with love and dance,
A slightly "Dirty" encounter, by chance.

She was rich and he did the foxtrot,
Wanting to learn, she asked, he taught.

When Daddy found out, disappointed was he,
Making the handsome dancer flee.

But he soon came back to prove his affection,
And to a huge crowd, he declared his connection.

Then they danced – such a romantic gift
To the beat of the music they did the lift.

And in that moment I could nearly cry
For it made ME even want to fly.

We'll never know if he made her his wife,
But this is my rhyme, to have the "Time of my life".

The Rhymes They Are A Changin'

When I was a child, I'd write a rose was red,
Instead of changing much, I'd hardly look ahead.

When I was just a tween, I took rhythm from a story,
And everything started 'twas the night,
I was filled with so much glory.

When I became a freshman, I wrote about the dark,
Blackest night, and things that fight,
An emotional landmark.

Writing turned to breakups, sadness, pain & grief,
Next thing I knew it was cowboys, rodeo relief.

Love came ever after, and then curiosity,
Each kind of poem varied, as life was changing me.

And each bitter obstacle life threw in my way,
Was building a new landing place, every single day.

As life's experiences happened,
My words were rearranging,
Writing is a calling, my rhymes they are a changing.

Any Rhyme At All

A really fat cat sat ready to splat
A rat on a hat should be under the mat.

The who at the zoo blew a shoe through a flue
When truth is in view all rhymes what I'll do.

As I go in the snow, with cold on my toe,
I know that I'll grow as I go with the flow.

Doesn't matter how small, the wall, or the fall,
when the poetry calls, it's any rhyme at all.

Rhymes Stand Still

When counting down the seconds,
Time stands still.
When waiting for a minute,
Time stands still.
When having an adventure,
Time speeds by,
It's a matter of perspective,
When time does fly.

When you were ever younger,
And were waiting,
Patiently looking forward, frustrating,
It always seemed extended
The waiting never ended.

Yet now that I am older,
Haven't got the will,
To wish the past was present,
Time stands still.

Sign of the Rhymes

When a cat and a rat sit together on a mat,
You know it's a sign of the rhymes.

When a hog on a jog, stops to sit on a log, (by a frog)
You know it's a sign of the rhyme.

When a black duck named Jack, looking for a small
Snack, ransacks his lunch pack, and finds out he can't
Quack, you know it's a sign of the rhymes.

When your date is at eight and you're gonna be late
It frustrates you to wait, for your straight talk
Roommate, that isn't great....

When you dread what you said, when Fred ran ahead,
As you wrongly misled with the words that you spread,

When you gawk at the clock as you walk and you talk
To a hawk who's in shock at the traffic gridlock,

And you moan and you groan at the cost of your
Loan, and you know, to postpone with your friend on
the phone until you're alone in the proper time zone,

When you just have to face, you've lost all your
Grace, and you race to retrace, the misplaced
Suitcase, you know, yes you know, it's a sign, a big
sign, of the ever changing, sign of the rhyme.

Strange Rhymes

My mother one time told me,
Or maybe more, I think,
That I'd not be allowed home,
If I colored my hair pink.

My mother also told me,
No tattoos would mar my skin,
That desecrating my body
Was a scriptural sin.

That also went for piercings,
Although I did my ears,
She did hers, so I did,
Her warnings were not fears.

And I have never done it,
No coloring, tattoos or rings,
But not because of her warnings,
I didn't want those things.

I'm not saying that you shouldn't,
You can do with what you want.
I just want to see who I am,
When a mirror, I'm in front.

Rhyme Machine

If I had a rhyme machine, where would I go?
I think to a world made of squishy play-dough.

If I had a rhyme machine, what would I do?
I'd look into the future, and get a preview.

If I had a rhyme machine, what would I learn?
Anything I wanted, until I'd return.

A rhyme machine is anything, the future, the past,
It's every question answered, anything that's asked.

It's a book of possibilities, wrapped in a rhythm song,
It sticks with you forever, even all along.

A rhyme machine in verse, is exactly what you need,
To bounce along a journey,
And imagine you've been freed.

Breakfast Rhyme

It's early in the morning, and when I do wake up,
the only thing I think about is coffee in my cup.

I'll drink my cup of coffee until it is no more,
Then I get to work, many hours before,

My stomach begins grumbling, ready for some food
And by then I must admit that I'm only in the mood

For something very quick & easy, speedy ready, too,
No eggs & bacon, toast & jam, cereal is what I'll do.

If I would have put some forethought
Pancakes would be great,
But my blood sugar's dropping,
Anything else is way too late.

Waffles with some syrup,
An omelet, oh my yes,
But the time that it would take
Is quite the long process.

No, I'll have to stick with cereal,
And eat it up quite quick.
It's no gourmet breakfast,
But it's my go to pick.

STORY TIME Poems

Once Upon A Rhyme

Once upon a rhyme, in a city far away,
There grows a lot of buildings,
Where children cannot play.

There are hardly any trees to climb,
No grass to cool our feet,
The midday sun beats on the concrete
And radiates such heat.

But then our little hero,
Moves from that noisy place,
Chooses a new life,
To leave the harsh rat race.

While simpler times are present,
And nature's all around,
Many opportunities
Can simply not be found.

But you'll not hear complaining,
I'm happy with my choice.
The quiet gave me the opportunity,
To finally find my voice.

Why Did the Cow Jump
Over the Moon?

Why did the cow jump over the moon,
I saw the book and asked.
"Guess you'll have to read the book",
My mother quickly tasked.

So in my arms the book was held
As we stood to wait in line,
I figured since it was a children's book,
The cow would turn out fine.

But the question remained, why, oh why,
Would the cow even be this crazy?
And what would the lack of gravity do,
To the milk inside Miss Daisy?

Would she make it, would she get stuck,
What if she's trapped on the moon?
I thought about her being stuck up there,
Worried all afternoon!

At last I sat my new book down
And opened up the cover,
And a book reader I became that day,
A reader and book lover!

Written for Preston

It's Fun to Have Fun

It's fun to have fun, and to be carefree.
It's a joyous feeling to feel such glee.

I like to laugh and dance for a while,
It makes me happy so I can smile.

It's the meaning of life, nothing too odd,
Appreciate what's there, cheer and applaud.

It's positive emotion, a sign of good health,
It's an inner feeling of success and wealth.

You don't have to be rich, to be outdone,
Appreciate life, enjoy and have fun,

Written for Melba

Uncaged

I've never had a pet bird, although I know a few.
When I hear them sing, I wonder if they're blue?

I remember I had an indoor cat,
Declawed and kind of lazy.
I never let him outside,
I felt that would be just crazy.

What if he got lost or hurt,
Would he know to come back home?
What if he got hit by a car,
If I let him out to roam?

No, I could never do it, but as he began to age,
I began to realize my home,
Had become his little cage.

He had all sorts of freedoms,
Any room he wanted to go,
Treats and all those feedings
Were his and, yes, I know...
That he surely did seem happy,
But he'd stare so longingly,
Out the picture windows,
The world was calling he.

So, one day I put him on a leash,
Which he didn't like one bit.
He refused to walk along, instead he'd rather sit.

But each day I gave him chances,
I took him out occasionally,
And after so much time,
He looked forward to them gratefully.

I'd leave him in the yard, on a tether that was tight,
And he looked so, so happy, like all would be alright.

I planted him some catnip, that patch he was fond of,
Uncaging him was a gift, that showed him my love.

Soon I took the biggest step, I took him off the line,
Do you know what happened? Everything was fine.

Over time he realized, as he laid out in the yard,
There were dangers just across the gate,
That could have been quite hard.

In his aging twilight days, he found such happiness,
Lying out in the sun, it filled him with such bliss.

This story may not work for you,
But if you've been engaged,
Consider setting others free, help them get uncaged.

Pictures to Remember

I know I say this often,
But when I was a child
Illustrations spoke to me,
I know because I smiled.

I had no one to read to me,
It's wasn't all that fun,
But looking at those pictures
Helped me one-by-one.

That little engine trying,
Those words I never read,
But as I flipped each page,
The story in my head,
For the most part all it said,
He tried and tried again,
With a smile plastered on his face,
He lifted high his chin.

When the missing piece was lonely,
Looking to find his home,
He wandered through the story,
So he wouldn't be alone.

I don't recall the message,
No words inside my brain,
But the simple illustrations,
Showed he tried and tried again.

I had a book about a unicorn,
"Morgan and Me" was the title,
Another one I never read,
But my imagination went wild.

The sweetest little princess,
Well, she was surely me,
And that unicorn she made friends with,
Was how it was meant to be.

I think that's why I write children's books,
Because they free my mind.
Yes the words are important,
But the illustrations all aligned.

Maybe I missed my childhood,
No adventures did I take,
No lifelong friends within the pages,
Did I ever get to make.

Yet, I also think that made me,
Into who I am today,
Because in my mind those pictures,
Opened up the way.

Never mattering to me
The simplicity or the splendor,
Each children's book important,
If it had pictures to remember.

Me Too Stew

On a cold winter's night Hamilton found
His cupboards were empty, there was no food around.

He went to his friends, they had nothing to spare,
There wasn't much left for them anywhere.

They wanted to help him, Hamilton knew,
But he was gonna go hungry, didn't know what to do.

Ah-ha, an idea popped into his head,
He figured out how to get everyone fed!

He gathered a cauldron as big as could be,
Then started a fire everyone could see.

They all came to watch this young little troll,
As he stirred and sniffed at his boiling bowl.

"What's that?" they asked with curious wonder.

"Me Too Stew." Tummies growled like thunder.

"If only I had a carrot or two..."

"I've got a carrot!" Beni Bunny came through.

"An onion? A potato?"

"I've got something to add."

"Me too!" "Me too!" They added quite glad.

They ran to their homes, grabbed what they could.
Threw it into the water and it smelled really good.

Within a few minutes, the stew was complete,
It was filled to the rim, and there was plenty to eat.

Everyone had some, there was more to be shared,
The evening was saved, with all who cared.

This story was originally published in the Hamilton Troll Cookbook copyright 2017. There is also a slightly animated video on YouTube and Hamilton Troll TV.

Candy Lake (Canyon Lake)

We're gonna go see Gramma, she lives at the lake,
A magical place to visit, that's even better than cake!

From the start of the day, as the sun starts to rise,
You see pink and blue icing throughout the skies.

She cooks up some pancakes, whipped cream and all,
Then our adventure begins, we all have a ball.

From her house, there's a field,
All scattered with Skittles,
Colorful flowers and critters
Looking for vittles.

There are birds on the trees, a musical treat,
You hand feed the deer who are timid but sweet.

From the tops of the trees
You see the sun rising up,
And I gaze at the beauty,
Drinking milk from my cup.

I see blue-purple hills, like cupcakes and such
Cotton candy clouds I just want to touch.

And then there's the lake a colorful blue,
And do you know what it's filled with?
Well I think I do...

They're blueberry Jelly Bellies and oh how they glitter
Like sugar on gramma's Apple Betty Fritters.

From a distance you see speed boats
Zoomin' 'cross the lake,
And my imagination soars
With the stories that I make.

Squishy Gummy Bears on the water as they play,
They're having so much fun throughout the day.

There are white Lifesavers that hang from the boat,
And help as they swim and keep them afloat.

And at the end of the day as the sun's going down,
The magic continues there's no time to frown.

Starbursts and Sweet Tarts fill up the night
Like a Halloween bucket full of sweets and delight.

And I fall fast asleep like an over-filled fruitcake
I dream about tomorrow at Gramma's Candy Lake.

Written for Carol

Do Aliens Exist?

Maybe I am crazy, or hopeful or just twisted,
But I'd like to think that aliens actually existed.

Not so they'd attack us, Hollywood drives fears.
Because I'd like to meet them, be scientific peers.

To those who don't believe, that is fine with me,
It's quite an extensive universe, wouldn't you agree?

To be the only life forms, seems odd and kind of skewed,
A narrow unopen mind, is how I might conclude.

I believe it'd be prideful to think them humanoid,
Sorry to anyone whom I have annoyed.

But what is the problem if they don't stand upright,
What if they'd wings and like a bird could take flight?

What if they were furry, like a dog, mouse or cat?
Would that offend us, what's wrong with that?

Would we not take them seriously if they traveled here?
Would they need to look like us, in order to be sincere?

I believe there's something else, what I do not know.
But I hope when they appear, that we will all forgo
Our pessimistic fears, our response of fight or flight,
And be welcoming and hopeful, to do what is right.

No Happy Endings

It occurred to me the other night
While watching a TV show,
That even when an episode ends,
No matter how it'd go,
Whether a happy moment
Or a cliff hanger to hang on,
There are no happy endings,
Because life always goes on.

Unless we're talking death,
Which no matter what is sad,
You really can't be happy,
They're gone, and that is bad.

And when you watch a movie,
And the orchestra starts up,
You must take into account,
Number 2 might get picked up.

So it may seem like a downer,
But if you're not pretending
As long as you're alive,
There is no happy ending.

INSPIRATIONAL
Poems

There's No Rhyme Like the Present

Don't look to the future, it will never arrive,
You may not make it, to get there alive.

Don't look to the past, it's over with now,
Be happy you made it, you survived somehow.

Look to the present, it is your gift,
Bow your head low, and give thanks to lift.

For today is your day, to succeed in life,
Take each moment today, don't live it in strife.

There's no rhyme like the present,
Because it's today,
Give thanks to the Lord in every way.

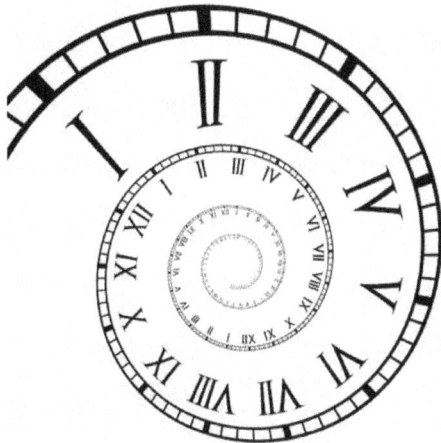

The Power of Prayer

My life was about living,
Every day about the same.
Nothing special to report,
Because He didn't know my name.

I was lonely and quite hungry,
Though I didn't know what for.
'Cause I hadn't been to church,
So I didn't know the Lord.

When I did attend I went for food,
Friendship and to sing.
The sermons in between were just,
Filling for this thing.

I may have kept attending,
For wrong mistaken reasons,
But at least I was in church through many,
Many seasons.

I had heard the stories, bowed my head,
But never really prayed.
Belief was unbelievable,
My soul was never swayed.

Yet that was when the trials came,
Such turmoil in my life.
My mother had been murdered,
And it caused me so much strife.

I was spiraling down a rabbit hole
That got darker by the day,
And that was when the Bible Group
Asked if they could pray.

They placed their hands upon me,
And asked our Lord to claim
My heart, my hope, my soul, my faith,
For me to know His name.

And in that moment of grief and pain,
I was weak enough to feel,
A soul's embrace that felt so warm,
My Lord became quite real.

He showed me love that I could sense,
Its power came from higher.
He showed me signs that He was there.
He filled my soul with fire.

When I look back along life's path,
My memories seem dark.
I had walked throughout my life,
Without an inkling of His spark.

Now each day I wake up knowing,
that He is part of me.
My roots are set, my trunk is tall.
I'm branches of His tree.

I'm reaching out in hopes
To fill my readers with my passion,
Testifying God's great love
Is full of such compassion.

He helped me through my rabbit hole.
He's with me everywhere.
My Christian soul is shining bright,
Thanks to the Power of Prayer.

*When life gets
too hard to stand...*

Kneel

God Thinks I'm Grand!

1 John 4:7 *(NIV)*
Dear friends, let us love one another,
for love comes from God. Everyone who
loves has been born of God and knows God.

I love, therefore I'm loved,
I take those words to heart
For love hath dost been mine,
Always, from the start.

I may have felt alone,
You may have felt it, too.
But love was always yours,
His love is always true.

He sent his only Son,
To take away our sins,
And that was how this love,
Was presented and begins.

I may not know enough,
My life may not be planned.
All I know is this,
God thinks that I am grand!

Distant Rainbows

Life is not easy, it is full of despair,
Just taking a step, problems are there.

No matter the distance you're due to roam,
You're gonna get rain at work or at home.

The rain might be light, the wind just a breeze
Nothing severe, no choppy seas.

But then comes a storm so dark and so rough,
The wind and the hail, the lightning's enough.

And it keeps pouring down, drowning your hope,
Flushed down the river, losing grip on your rope.

Damage is happening, faith tested hard,
Innocence shattered, your soul has been scarred.

It feels like forever since the sun has come out,
You're tired of worrying, you plead and you shout.

They say there's a rainbow, always, the end,
But it takes a completion and a specific bend.

With just the right lighting, all things aligned,
The clouds and the sun and all things combined.

You don't always see it, it's sometimes not there,
And you feel with those storms, well that isn't fair.

Just cuz the sun's out, doesn't mean that it's done,
The rain may be stopped, but you haven't won.

You may feel exhausted, you've had too much pain,
But it doesn't always get rainbows after the rain.

More showers coming, more dark days await,
They just don't care, if too much is on your plate.

It's meant to challenge, it's meant to be hard,
You're meant to learn and be on your guard.

Because when it is finished and when you are done,
The storms will cease, and you'll see the sun.

The evening will pass, morning will rise,
Clouds will part and you'll see the skies.

The sun will shine, on a dark, dark blue,
And that's when you'll know, your rainbow is due.

Colossians 3:17 *(NIV)*

And whatsoever ye do in word or deed,
do all in the name of the Lord Jesus,
giving thanks to God and the Father by Him.

I thank the Lord for blessings
He's bestowed within the years,
From the joys of daily wonders
To the sorrows and the tears.

He's guided me and helped me
Along life's narrow lane,
And now it is my turn,
Please, let me explain:

There are missions to support
With benefits so grand,
Scholarships for women
And minds we can expand.

Food and clothes to help the needy,
Children to support,
Disaster relief and materials,
And everything of the sort.

There's so much we can do,
So much to achieve,
That's why we collect,
So others can receive.

I give because I'm called to
Because He makes it known,
I give because I've prospered
My spirit it has grown.

I give because I'm blessed
So many things in life are mine.
I give because I want to;
For His glory is divine.

He giveth me so much,
So now it is my turn.
Let's pledge this year for Him,
And what we can return.

Forever Love

And there was light...
A miraculous light,
A light of true colors,
Of purples & gold,
And blues & pinks,
And greens & such.

And it spoke to me.
It gave me every answer
I ever needed to hear.

And I knew then,
That it was He.

He had answered my prayers,
He had given me the chance,
And it was He who was in my life.

Now, Before and Tomorrow,
Forever Love,
In the Eyes of the Beholder.

Poetry in Motion

A butterfly flies and flutters it's wings,
A teeny tiny bird, chirps and sings.

The wind blows the leaves, they dance in the air,
It's poetry in motion, all I do is stare.

A ballet dancer spinning, a pirouette,
The curves and the speed of a red Corvette.

Water how it moves, it trickles or falls,
So many animals, their coos and calls.

Looking down at earth, the lights from the sky,
The colors all blur, as if they could fly.

Clouds how they move, the shapes and the colors,
A sunset, a sunrise, every natural wonders.

Choreography of life, the beauty of the ocean,
Take a look and see, poetry in motion.

Moving A Mountain

I was once given a spoon, and then I was asked
To go move a mountain, that was my task.

Go move a mountain, from one side to the next?
I must admit that I was somewhat perplexed.

I asked how to do that, appeal on my face,
They said I could do it, as long as I had faith.

Faith will move mountains, that I was told,
I must admit, the theory didn't have me sold.

But I took my small teaspoon, and I started to dig,
One little teaspoon didn't seem so big.

This was my task, I wouldn't dispute,
So step after step I kept on my pursuit.

Day after day, I kept on digging,
And began imagining a better rigging.

I invented ways to make my job easier,
Which I must admit, kept me so much busier.

I grew, I got better, had good days and blah,
But no matter what, do you know what I saw?

One side getting smaller, other side grew,
I was getting it done, working it through.

Each day I succeeded in moving the dirt,
Advancing my goal, like a big expert.

So, at the end of my life, I looked back and caught,
I had moved a mountain – that's a lot!

They said to have faith, it would get me through,
With patience and persistence, who woulda knew?

It may seem obscure, someone coming in now,
They won't see success, they may not say, "Wow!"

But in my life time, I'll know I got it done,
No matter how difficult, without the fun.

Others may scoff, ignore or forbid,
But to me and my Lord we know what we did.

Innocence

Innocence of a child, should be theirs as long as they
Can hold it in their heart song, forever this I pray.

Innocence of a first love, such blinded hope and will, I
Pray your love is good to you, it always shows goodwill.

The innocence of adulting, starting out on your first path,
I pray your boss is kind, never fall prey to the warpath.

But innocence doesn't get to stay,
At some point your life will change,
Something bad will happen,
Words will be exchanged.

Trust will leave your heart, your soul turns dark as night,
Shake your head with grief, that nothing will be right.

Don't let the bad times mold you, don't let them ruin what
 innocence you held on to, kick hate in the gut.

Innocence is all yours, it never goes away,
It's with you every night, and sticks there every day.

It's your happiness and calmness, your feelings of
Content, it never goes away, no matter the event.

You can call it back to you, it's yours and yours alone,
Call back your innocence to stay, claim it as your own.

A Heart of Light

For those who know me, delight they know,
My heart's like a light bulb bright it'll glow.

A radiant warmth that's open to love,
A brilliant array I share from above.

My heart's like an abstract, colors galore,
That flood through a canvas, dreaming of more.

A vivid display that erupts like a splash,
That light up a room as quick as a flash.

I'm a soul you should know, not just 'cause I write,
I have so much to offer, like a heart full of light.

Godspeed

An expression of good wishes,
They say to astronauts.
But where did the phrase come from?
Spilled out of my thoughts.

So as any author, curious, I
Researched origins,
And found that 15h century
Is where the phrase begins.

Middle English God Spede,
Is how it was once spelled,
Blessing one's prosperity,
A journey they'd upheld.

Not swiftness, but goodbye,
God be with ye, too.
Because back then on a journey,
You might not make it through.

So God be with you daily,
This journey will be long.
May you prosper and be well,
With prayers to keep you strong.

Good will through your adventure,
May you have all that you'll need,
And may everything stay well with you,
Take care my love – Godspeed.

Dream Big

Dream big or go home, but that is not right,
Home's where the heart is, where the fire ignites.

Dream big and work hard, is that a cliché?
Is that really true, the only way?

Dream big and think bigger, the results will appear,
You'll lead the way in this first frontier.

Dream big and believe, that is all optional,
If you put your mind to it, anything's possible.

Arms Wide Open

If you want to be my friend, all you need is ask,
I'll embrace you in my heart of hearts,
As if it is my task.

I'll give you every chance at it, trust that I'm all in,
I'll be there until the end of time,
Through thick and then through thin.

I'll never take for granted, although I may forget,
To call and be there for you,
But don't you ever fret.

If you call my line, I'll answer, always be there for you,
Won't ask you for a favor,
If it's something I won't do.

Forever is a long time, but that is what I'm hoping
Friendship is my present
I accept with arms wide open.

I am a Sinner

I am a sinner, I cannot lie,
A criminal I'm not, and will deny.

No laws I've fractured,
No commandments I've broken,
And yet, even that, is a sin I've spoken.

I'll admit it confused me,
"while we were yet sinners".
I'm a good person, I'm part of the winners.

I don't smoke, but I drink, and yes, that's okay,
He turned wine from water, so what can I say?

I haven't killed, no humans I've taken,
But bugs, well that's different,
Those lives I've forsaken.

I try not to cuss, but life can get tough,
And those words when they come,
Well, enough is enough.

I've spoken in vain, those phrases I shouldn't ,
But I'm only human - an angel sure wouldn't.

I'll never cheat on games, life or my love,
I'm proud of myself, I'll stand above.

I'll claim it all day, because I am good,
But a sinner I am, and repent it, I should.

In a Whisper

The world is always yelling,
They scream and honk their horns,
Piercing sounds at night,
Like a rose's piercing thorns.

The loudest of all shouts,
The roar of every message,
Can take someone I care about,
Right up to the edge.

The ruckus is unbearable,
How can I ever hear,
The one that I am longing for,
The one that I want near.

I'd rather shut it out,
The blast of turbulence,
I'd rather hear the quiet
On this side of the fence.

A boisterous bewailing, is like a constant hum,
Banging at the silence, piercing like a drum.

The quietness of life is more than I can figure,
I declare it from the mountains, as I prefer a whisper.

Written for Jerre

Water

Water is quite the substance,
The things that it can do,
Go from liquid, solid and gas,
Chemistry, it's true.

Water creates grand canyons,
Brings life to a dried up plant,
When still or hardly moving,
Its ripples can enchant.

It's hot water that makes the kettle sing,
The steam evaporates fast,
It steeps and makes great flavors,
When you combine it with your past.

A pot of boiling water, softens a potato to mash
Can also harden an egg, and it'll do it in a flash.

It proves it's not what you're made of,
Your life gives so many chances,
Water gives you hope,
It's not the circumstances.

CHALLENGE & CHANGE
Poems

Reflections

Reflections from the surface, a light reflected back,
A mirror shows reflections, even if it's cracked.

A million pieces jagged, reflections are still there,
Reflections shall display your feelings, if you care.

If you look at your reflection, what will you see?
Are you happy with what's there, do you agree?

Be content with your reflection,
It is who you portray
If you want to make it better,
Then be better every day.

If you want love, give love,
If you want happiness well,
Open your heart to the future,
And reflect what you want to tell.

If you want to be respected,
Mirror what you want,
Share what you desire,
Be forward and upfront.

Be a reflection of what you want to see
In him and her and thee,
You'll get what you return to them,
Reflections shown of me.

Change...

Change is quite disheartening,
It's worrisome and hard,
Change can be incredulous,
It can catch you off your guard.

A revision of your life's plan,
Your future variable,
But change can instead be great,
And somewhat pleasurable.

Change is not expected,
You usually cannot plan,
And that's what throws you out of sorts,
It's not how you began.

A contradicting force,
That turns over all designs,
A substitute for plans,
That reshapes all the lines.

Don't let all of this change
Fill you with such strife.
You were born with the ability,
To change someone's life.

That's right...

When change comes at you harshly,
Maybe someone's aim,
Was exactly what you needed,
They help to change the game.

Maybe metamorphosis
Translates to someone's lead,
An intentional distraction,
Was exactly what you need.

The time to challenge forethoughts,
To strengthen inner will,
Maybe change is wanted,
Change won't keep you still.

You have the chance to grab it,
Held within your palms,
Every step you take,
Lets go of changing bombs.

You may not know you did it,
They may not know their task,
But change is just an angel,
Hidden by a mask.

Persistence

There are times in life, when issues come your way,
And it's up to you, to pass or play.

If you accept that challenge, and you face it strong,
It'll be taken care of before too long.

Persistence is trying, and repeated failures,
It's a speeding train with so many derailleurs.

It's a dispute or headache with a puzzle to solve,
It's a kind of freedom when it's been resolved.

No matter how difficult, the problem seems,
The level of complications at all extremes,

An endless attempt to figure it out,
It'll rattle your cage, and cause you to doubt.

The situation dire, struggling hard,
Persistence is acceptance with all regard.

Accept all your failures, and accept overall,
That to win at this game, is for the long haul.

An attempt at failure, as an attempt to succeed,
For when it comes to you, it's just what you need.

You'll continue trying, and if you do fail,
You'll keep on trying, to no avail.

Because when you get, an impossible task won,
You'll be glad you took it, success when it's done.

What better feeling, to know for sure,
You faced that challenge and did endure.

Because those who give up, they'll never win.
Persistence pays off, so hold up your chin.

Waiting for Life to Start

I've been waiting for my life to start
For half my life so far,
Waiting for the next great day
That sets the higher bar.

A weekend, a vacation,
A milestone to play,
But at the end of that moment
I'm looking towards the next day.

It occurred to me that at this rate
I'll never find my joys,
That waiting for the next big thing
Is one of life's cruel ploys.

I'll never find my happy
In a world where we all wait,
I must wait until the end
And that'll be the greatest date.

I'm waiting to meet my Maker
Whenever He's ready for me,
He's the reason I'm here
And feeling less than free.

So, I'll take each moment as it comes,
Broken as each section
Cause I've realized what I'm waiting for,
I'm waiting for perfection.

I Can and I Will

Put your mind to it, is what they would say,
And so, with some worry, I chose that one day.

I decided my goal, my aspect in life,
No matter the obstacles, worries or strife.

I put my mind to it, and yes, it is hard,
Working so long, getting hurt and scarred.

But I'll keep persisting, my dream will be mine.
All will work out, everything is just fine.

Will I do everything, to utilize my skill?
You better believe I can, & you better believe I will!

We Only Have What We Give...

I was born a disappointment,
A reason, not a plan.
A bill to be collected on,
That's how I began.

I soon became a burden,
A reason just to fight.
I was guilty of living,
My judgement was their spite.

In rationale it's crazy,
To take on that kind of pain.
The guilt is not my own,
But that's what's been ingrained.

My beginning taught me hatred,
Blame and inner doubt.
And if I would have listened,
I'd might have fallen out.

But I never took their problems,
And made them all my own.
I knew that I was different,
That I was not alone.

Yes, I may be human,
And there are things this life can't do.
There are aspects of my past,
I refuse to give light to.

But I didn't let them stop me,
From being who I am.
I still tend to lean towards good,
They weren't my diagram.

I want my life to be happy,
Full of love and fun.
And I know that there is darkness,
Before the morning sun.

There may be limitations,
But my life I chose to live.
Day by day I work it,
We only have what we give.

Don't See Through Me,
See Me Through

I see you sit there, you hide in your skin,
You see everyone, but this way you won't win.

You're shy and demure, and modest reserved,
This way of living, how well has it served?

I used to be like that, humbled with fear,
So cautious of speaking when someone was near.

It left me alone, friendless and lost.
It won't help you - loneliness will cost.

So when I see you alone, looking so much like me,
I remember my feelings; how I used to be.

And I know what you need, I needed it to.
I want to show you just what to we can do.

I'll walk up to you, say hi, share my name,
Ask you some questions, hope you'll do the same.

Break you out of your shell, you're safe by my side,
Please don't revert, go back and hide.

I'm here to express love, I've learned what to do,
Don't see through me, please see me through.

Go On With Your Glad Self!

A boisterous laughter
Erupts within the room,
It wafts in the air
Like a fragrant perfume.

It startles the crowd
Make the others want in,
They smile, you shine,
It's a perfect win-win.

When you have hope to share,
Don't keep to yourself,
Laugh and have fun,
Go on with your glad self!

Risk

It's hard to take risks, because you don't know
How it'll turn out, how it will go.

Should you jump in, with both feet and heart?
Should you be weary, right from the start?

Should you toe-test the waters, taste-test the meal,
Be open to anything, question how it may feel?

Risk is not easy, it's all the unknown.
If you don't take risks, you'll never get grown.

And sometimes it hurts and you might get harmed,
But you'll never know if you're always alarmed.

You've got to let go, and accept the risk,
Pour in the ingredients, and stir with a whisk.

And when the mixing is done, I think you'll agree,
There's a better you, that's a guarantee.

The Children

Children are our future, and sometimes that worries me.
Can they grasp what's needed to keep us living free?

Can they understand, we'll need them very soon.
It's very much expected, although not opportune.

They'll need to make decisions, our future's in their hands.
So many things are needed, we've all got our demands.

How will they know to do right, the choices they will make,
Will cost them & their offspring, with every step they take.

When they're at their end, like one day we will be,
Will they look back & wonder if all this stuff should be?

How can we tell them, to explain the cost of life?
How will we teach them, to deal with all this strife?

What can we do now, to keep them moving strong?
How can we teach them, to instill what's right or wrong?

The children are our future, we'll put them to the test.
All that we can hope, is that we all did do our best.

Written for Alysia

Why Can't We Just Get Along?

Why does everybody fight, why can't we get along?
What if neither one of you
Is completely right or wrong?

Why can't we find the chalk line,
See the grey area in place?
We are all so similar, why get in each other's face?

So what if your thinking differs,
If your beliefs don't mesh with mine,
Why can't we think differently,
Won't everything be just fine?

I don't have a problem with your choices,
You get to live with them.
If you find it makes you happy,
Who am I to condemn?

I really care about you,
I don't want us to have any spats,
Let me like my dogs, and you can like your cats.

Written for Joyce

Illusions

An optical illusion is one of my favorite things,
To see a still picture moving, imagination it brings.

Colors making shapes, the opposite in your mind,
I love to see what happens, to see what I can find.

Drawings that look real, but are physically impossible,
Look like they could work, they almost could be plausible.

Illusions make my brain spin, I love the way they feel,
Even when magicians and their magic looks so real.

You know that it's impossible, authentically not true,
But I love to watch them, I watch until they're through.

Sometimes I can see it, figure out the trick,
Other times I'm dumbfounded, they really are that slick.

And, yes, I know it's fake, I don't have delusions.
All I know is that I love them,
Those wonderful illusions!

Written for Ron

No Rhyme or Reason

If I analyze the scene
Try to figure out what's wrong,
Speculate and deliberate,
All while staying strong.

I might contemplate the version,
Study every word,
Rationalize the fiction,
While feeling most absurd.

But reflecting fabrication,
Deducing nothing good.
Falsehoods running rampant,
Dripping where I stood.

Though I'll resolve to accept it,
Even though it feels like treason,
Having nothing to write about,
Feels like no rhyme or reason.

The Help

She's 85 or thereabout
Still on the go without a doubt
Acts young and keeps on ticking
Thinks like a teen and keeps on kicking.

So it makes sense that she she'd need a hand,
To see to her plans all come out grand,
To oversee and help to guide,
So every party will present her pride.

It's important to know she's got a friend,
Who'll be there helping throughout the end,
To assist with cleanup, cooking too,
To do all that she used to do.

You keep her young, you keep her going,
You keep the beverages, cool and flowing.
Whether she says it, or whether not,
Please know you are valued more than a lot.

Helping out is not all you do,
But it's you who's there and gets her through.

Written for Terry

Barefoot Hopscotch on Asphalt

I was outside playing, when I took off my shoes
to walk through the grass, was what I did choose.

The cool spears of green, tickled my toes,
And yet there were lurkers, within the shadows.

Little did I know, someone spotted my shoes.
Would they give them back? No, they'd refuse.

"We dare you to do something crazy for them."
So unfortunately, I was at their beckon whim.

Looking to their left, they saw three girls playing.
Chalk lines were drawn, Hopscotch displaying.

"If you play Hopscotch on this burning hot asphalt,
We'll give you your shoes back, win like default."

So, what could I do, I was good at the game.
I hadn't thought of the burning hot pain,
I leapt on the first square, but before I could hop,
My brain screamed out – whoa, man – please stop!

I fell back to the grass, my butt landed hard,
I was grateful for the coolness of this green yard.

I blew at my bare soles, already hot pink,
This was a dare, I'd have to rethink!

But the boys egged me on, placed my shoes on ten.
All I had to do, was hop and win.

I could deal with the blisters, get past the burn,
Then it'd be worth it, to watch their turn.

I sucked up my bravery, took a deep breath,
THIS would not be the time for death!

I was gonna get them, and prove I could do it,
But I did say a prayer, asking help I'll admit.

And just as I stood, a tiny cloud showered
And sprinkled cool rain. Oh, was I empowered!

I grinned at the boys, who looked so shocked,
And that Hopscotch game, oh yes – I rocked!

I grabbed my shoes and no pain had I -
Thanks to a rain cloud within the sky.

Written for Tim

Growing Old and Growing Gray

No, I'm not there yet, no coloring for me,
I've only seen a few white strands,
So I am still carefree.

I don't have any wrinkles,
My joints don't creak too much,
So I'll not be complaining
About growing old and such.

But it doesn't mean I see it, in friends I care for so,
Bright white heads of fluffy hair,
It sets their eyes aglow.

Yet they take strides from it, laugh at ailments too,
Slowing down is not in store,
With so much they want to do.

There's shopping, groups and wine clubs,
Parties, feasts and church,
Old age is just a mindset, won't leave 'em in a lurch.

So just 'cause I'm growing older
And soon I may even turn gray.
It's not going to be a downer,
When it's Time to Have a FUN Day!!!

Written for LaVerne

Weakness...

I am weak, and yet I am strong,
I've always known it, all along.

It's a choice to be hopeful, allows me to care,
When I scream or cry, when it's too much to bear,

It shows you I'm human, but I am not weak.
It's an inner strength, to turn that cheek.

Open and vulnerable, and not so protected,
My heart may be hurt, but I am respected.

I am alive and I am not broken
By those words of hate that others have spoken.

They make me stronger, they ignite a spark
That illuminates my path, right out of the dark.

You see I keep going, and that's the design.
No matter the obstacle, I will be fine.

Because I may cry, I may look broken,
But the strength in my heart ,has just been awoken.

MUSICAL Poems

Yes, I love writing lyrics!
Yes, I hear the music in my head.
Yes, you can sing them too!

Rhyme in a Bottle

If I could put rhymes in a bottle,
The first one I'd like to share,
Is to live every day
To the fullest, I say
Just because I want you know I care.

If I could make rhymes last forever,
If rhymes could bring smiles to you,
I'd rhyme every moment, in hopes that it would,
Make you want, to rhyme with me too.

But there never seems to be enough rhymes
To express the love, I feel inside, for everyone.
I've rhymed enough, to know that I might
Lose the words, that I don't use
It'll be done.

If I had a book just for rhyming,
And poems I've written for you,
The book would be heavy with so many words
That I hope one day will break through...

But there never seems to be enough rhymes
To express the love, I feel inside, for everyone.
I've rhymed enough, to know that I might
Lose the words, that I don't use
It'll be done.

Good Rhymes

Good rhymes – anytime you read it baby,

Good rhymes – anytime you need a break.

Good rhymes – when you're ready to read poetry

Rhyming is life's blood, won't you agree?

Poems bring life to a story –

Rhyming is always the key –

Customary rhyme time,

Good rhymes – Rhythm working full time

Good rhymes – Stanzas all by design

Good rhymes –

So very happy to read them – Good rhymes.

Let the Good Rhymes Roll

Let the good rhymes roll,
Let them make you aglow.
Let the good rhymes roll,
Let the poetry flow.

Let them raise your spirits high,
Let them take you into the sky!

Let the good rhymes roll,
Let the good rhymes roll,
Let the good rhymes roll,

Let the words be good,
They'll inspire your heart.
Write the phrases bold,
Hope they set you apart.

Let them raise your spirits high,
Let them take you into the sky!

Let the good rhymes roll,
Let the good rhymes roll,
Let the good rhymes roll,

Baby One More Rhyme

Oh maybe, baby, how was I supposed to write,
When something wasn't rhyming.

—

Oh maybe baby,
I shouldn't have stopped my rhyme
'Cuz now I've lost my rhythm.

—

Spare me so I can be carefree
Sharing, cuz I need to write now – just because –

My lack of rhyme is bugging me (maybe)
I recognize my quandary (quandary)

When I'm not rhyming I lose my way,
Give me a rhyme…

Rhyme it baby one more time!

If I Could Turn Back Rhyme

If I could turn back rhyme,
If I could overturn,
I'd reverse all those stanzas that forced rhyme,
So you'd learn...

I can't explain those lines that almost rhyme,
I know it's hard, but it is worth the climb,
Rhyming is tough, but it comes from deep inside
And if it's done right, it's sublime!

I didn't really mean to force it,
no bad rhyme is really worth it,
I know it made you cringe, but baby,

If I could turn back rhyme,
If I could overturn,
I'd reverse all those stanzas that forced rhyme,
So you'd learn...

If I rewrote those words,
I know they'd rhyme just fine,
Then you'd love them, love them,
like you're meant to do.

If I could turn back rhyme...

Remember the Rhyme

Do you remember, when we spoke of words,
We were wannabe authors back then.
Do you remember, your book in your hands
Oh the joy we felt right then, and how great it was.

Do you remember your first book sale?
It was money in your palm.
Do you remember, your first review?
Five stars, how it felt like the bomb.

Bridge: Do you remember the rhyme
When it was so good?
Do you remember the rhyme
When it all worked out?
Do you remember the rhyme
When it was good?
Do you remember the rhyme?

Do you remember, how it used to flow,
Flowing from the pen to paper, flowed so fluidly.
Do you remember, all the things you wrote?
Oh those pages full, the time we'd devote.

Do you remember, back in the day,
When you always knew the way?
Do you remember, the dialog?
When your characters knew what to say and do.

Bridge again:

Too Much Rhyme on My Hands

I'm sitting at my desk, trying to type up a rhyme, and
I don't know what I am doing,
I've written a fun one, a harsh one, a dumb one and
Now I am stewing.

I've got to wonder if I'm out of words.
Yeah I wonder if those words are gone.

Well I'm so tired of writing, but not tired of living,
All those stories I dream up.
I want to go there all day and enact, and to play,
And I must do a backup.

I've got to wonder if it's good to be me?
Is it any wonder I get things done?

Is it any wonder I've got too much, X-X,
Rhyme on my hands,
And it's taking away from my writing time.
I've got too much, X-X, rhyme on my hands.
It's hard to believe, but it's true to me
I've got too much, XX-, rhyme on my hands,
And it's taking away, taking that time from me,
(too much rhyme on my hands)
At, bat, cat, fat, hat, that's
(too much rhyme on my hands)
I don't know what to do
(too much rhyme on my hands)…

Don't Go Breaking My Rhyme

Don't go breaking my rhyme.
   I couldn't rhyme, I tried.
But darling if I can't do it...
   Babe, you got it inside.

Don't go breaking my rhyme.
   Your poems speak to me.
So, if I can't rhyme no more...
   No way it would be.

Bridge: Ooh-noo, Nobody saw it.
      I couldn't write it,
    Life was black night.
      Ooh-hoo, Nobody saw it (nobody saw)
    My block it was real,
      It's just how I'd feel (just how I'd feel)

So don't go breaking my rhyme,
   I won't go breaking your rhyme,
Don't go breaking my rhyme.

And nobody knew it
   Cause nobody asked me,
But I made it through baby.
   I knew you could make it.

So don't try to break me,
   Rhymes put the light in my life.
They put the spark in your flame,
   I've got a new rhyme on the way. *(Bridge)*

The Habanero Pepper Pickle Eater

Well, I saw him moseying down the road.
He wore a poncho, hat with hair that flowed.
I began to giggle and I said ooh-eee,
"It's The Habanero Pepper Pickle Eater – See!"

He was a dark haired Habanero,
Hot Pepper Pickle Eater
(a dark haired, Habanero, Hot Pepper Pickle Eater)
A dark haired, Habanero, Hot Pepper Pickle Eater
Watching his mouth shoot flames *(woo-wee)*

Well he walked in the shop and sat on a chair.
I asked what he wanted, and everyone stared.
He answered quickly and kinda blunt
"You know exactly what I want!"

Well I brought out a tray and watched him start,
Sweat started pouring from every part.
His face turned red,
His head hung low,
We stared as he only had two to go!

He was the super crazy,
Habanero Pepper Pickle Eater
(the super crazy Habanero Pepper Pickle Eater)
The super crazy Habanero Pepper Pickle Eater
Sure sounds hot to me!

Written for Preston

New Doggy in the Doghouse

I want a new doggy for my doghouse,
Because my old dog ran away.
I want a new doggy for my doghouse,
A new dog so we can both play.

I guess I'll go check out the pet store,
Maybe the kennel or pound,
I'm hoping to find a new doggy,
So I'll have a friend to stick around.

I want a new doggy for my doghouse,
Because my old dog ran away.
I want a new doggy for my doghouse,
A new dog so we can both play.

I don't really care about its color,
It's fur length doesn't matter to me.
I just want a doggy who is friendly,
A dog who can be carefree.

I found a new doggy for my doghouse!
Oh, he sure made my day.
I found a new doggy for my doghouse,
And now we're gonna go out and play.

Written For Johnny

Flat Tire Blues

Riding my bike on a hot summer day,
Doin' what I like, lookin' like play,
Gonna pop me a wheelie,
Leave y'all in the dust -
When bang! It exploded,
Tire's a bust!

Now I've got the blues – oh yeah,
The flat tire blues.
I've got the blues, (like-pow!)
Flat tire blues.

Tube rattles off, like a straw paper wrapper,
The rim sure is bent,
Don't know what to do now.
Allowance is spent,
Gotta find a way to get back,
The road calls my name,
Walking'll kill me,
Just not the same.

So I've got the blues – Oh yeah,
The flat tire blues...
I've got the blues, (pow) Flat tire blues.

Written for Stefanie

FAMILY & FRIENDS
Poems

Angels are Mothers

There are Angels God puts on this Earth,
Who care for us and guide us.
You can feel their love and gentleness,
As they walk through life beside us.

They do great things for us every day,
They whisper in our ears.
They even hold us in their hearts,
When we are filled with fears.

They are always there to give a hug,
And try to make us smile.
They treat us with respect and love,
They treat us like their child.

God blessed me with an Angel,
I'm proud to call my own.
She's been with me throughout my life,
Been with me as I've grown.

She's guided me the best she can,
She's taught me like no other.
And I'm thankful I'm the lucky one,
Who gets to call her... MOTHER

Written for my Mom
on a Mother's Day so very long ago.

December 15, 1954 – July 11, 2008

Sisters in Anguish

Oh look at those shoes – oh my, they're so cute!
Look at those heels, I look so astute.
The leather, the lace, the cloth and the buckles,
"I can't wait to wear them!" each lady chuckles.

But lo – when you wear them,
Your head held up high,
You're feeling so proud of your excellent buy.
But as the day goes, each step wearies on,
You begin to consider these shoes are hell's spawn.

Your ankles are swelling, your dogs do they bark,
Your heels and your muscles shoot up like a spark.
You look forward to home time,
To kick off your shoes,
And walk in your slippers - Shoe Anguish Blues.

The very next morning the pumps call to you.
They're still so amazing, a beautiful shoe.
So like every woman, we forget all our pain.
We're sisters in anguish – yes, we are so vain.

Each step that we take, a reminder, a hint.
Every ooh and ahh - a valued compliment...
The emotions run wild, does it confuse?
Glance in a window – Oh, look at *those* shoes!

Sturdy as a Tree

Independence of mind and a little reserved,
Self-confident is what I've observed.

A majestic tower, roots planted firm,
You're like a tree and this I confirm:

Your sturdiness is far greater than mine,
You're proven to pass the test of time.

To brave the elements, standing firm and brave,
With gentle branches intent to save.

Your leaves they shelter, your limbs they reach,
Your years of knowledge, within you teach.

Your age and beauty, an approving smile,
You're like a tree, sit and stay awhile.

With love so bold you stand tall and grin,
The majestic tree alive within.

So enjoy this day as a tree does, always,
For this day is for you and your birthdays.

Quite a Pair

When I think to years so long ago,
When I was just a kid,
I remember many things 'bout you,
And what we always did.

I remember walking through the woods,
How I'd stay out there all day.
I remember how you'd sneak up on me,
And scare me as I play.

I remember going to the movies,
And then to "Mickey D's"
For a happy meal and playtime.
You'd do whatever I please.

Then I remember those trips home,
When Sunday rolled around.
I remember how you'd smile,
When mine turned upside down.

And you'd drive right down snake road,
Just to savor our last bit of time.
And that's when I'd realize, everything
Would be just fine.

I was Daddy's little girl,
I could do nothing wrong.
And I miss those days of carefree bliss
That I had all along.

And now that things are different,
All I have are memories,
Wonderful and precious, yet
Sometimes they tend to tease.

Of days that are long gone,
As life moves up and on,
And each darkened night
Fades to the soon approaching dawn.

As I grasp tight to olden times,
I look on to the future at hand.
Then I realize it's not over,
Our trip has just began.

So I look forward to more times ahead,
Where you and I will share,
Fun and enjoyment together,
Because we make quite a pair!

*Written for my Daddy
on a Father's Day so very long ago.*

December 23, 1953 – September 28, 2018

My Friend

It always seems to amaze me
How quickly change occurs,
Like a constant flowing river
Of near icy cold waters.

Like the tides change, bringing newness,
Like the wind blows in fresh air,
I know things never stay the same,
But this time's just not fair.

I feel like I just met you,
And now you move away.
I smile shyly knowing
That this is your last day.

I pray we'll keep in touch,
I pray, because of the past.
I'd say those things and try it,
But those things don't seem to last.

You're the first friend that I met here,
I cherish you a bunch.
And although our times been short,
Know, I love you very much.

Friendship to me is special,
For me it's really tough.
I either suffocate a friend,
Or don't give them quite enough.

To find someone I care about
Is the simplest job, of course.
To me, it's as simple as love,
For better or for worse.

I will always be here for you,
To talk, to listen, to write,
At the very least in spirit,
If I'm not in clear plain sight.

Email, write or call me,
I'll always lend an ear.
My schedules not so crazy,
You know I'm always here.

I know one day I'll visit you,
And you'll be back I'm sure.
All I hope is that our friendship lasts
The test of time, so pure.

As I end this thought, I know there's more,
So much there is to say,
But I'll leave that for another time,
Another friendly day.

I love you and I'll miss you.

Your Fishing Pole

There is something about you,
Something in your soul,
Something that seems to surround
Your fishing pole....

You moved to the coast,
Now that's no lie,
And we had a hard time
With that little goodbye.

But no need for heartache,
No need to console.
You had your boat
And your fishing pole.

You know every day
You go out to fish.
It's like a genie
Granting every little wish.

Every time that bobber
Goes out of control
We know you are happy
With your fishing pole.

Now on birthdays,
It's special out on the water.
I hear if you're there,
They'll jump for the slaughter.

You'll be piling them in,
Like your lucks on a roll.
Reeling them in,
With your fishing pole.

So, today of all days,
Take heed and relax.
Pack up a cooler,
With drinks and some snacks.

Put on your shoes,
And go take a stroll.
Down to your boat,
With your fishing pole.

Soggy Grape-Nuts

Breakfast is the most vital meal of the day,
At least that's what the parents always tend to say.

If you're lucky you get bacon,
Eggs and buttered toast,
Pancakes and/or waffles, I like those the most.

There's fruit and cream cheese Bagels,
Grits and shredded wheat,
I've never met a breakfast I wouldn't want to eat.

But the bestest and my favorite,
Is cereal Galore,
So many different flavors,
Cuisine that I adore.

There's Fruit Loops, Cap'n and Cocoa,
Pebbles, Puffs and crunch.
I could eat them dry or with milk,
Any type I'd love to munch.

But you'd stick with the basics.
No colors shapes or balls.
No marshmallows or berries, no frosting protocols.

You stuck with simple Grape-Nuts,
Every day for decades too.
You wouldn't even add berries,
It must have made you blue.

Because you'd pour your Grape-Nuts,
The milk you'd even add,
But then you'd go 'bout your morning
And leave them sitting - sad.

For hours they'd sit waiting,
A gloomy bowl of glum.
Soaking up the milk, making Goo of every crumb.

And when you'd return upstairs,
While standing at the sink,
You'd shovel down your Grape-Nuts -
To bowl, the spoon would clink.

And it always made me wonder,
Why Soggy Grape-Nuts where your meal?
The consistency of glue, what was the appeal?

But now that you are gone,
I think fondly of your choice.
And giggle with remembrance,
You lived - so I Rejoice.

Maybe one day soon, I'll try some Grape-Nuts too.
So I can pull a Grandpa, and for one day, be like you!

Written for Grandpa

June 14, 1924 – March 4, 2017

Joyful Barry

He'd leap from bed, his tail held high.
What to do today? The limit's the sky.

First there'll be breakfast, then maybe a ride?
Oh, how I love going outside!

Errands today? Oh, I sure love those!
Where we'll end up? Nobody knows.

I'll stand by the car, I won't even budge.
"Isn't this great?" I'll say with a nudge.

We'll go to the bank, and when we drive thru,
I get a cookie, Yes. Good boy. I do!

We went to DQ, ice cream I got.
I sure love ice cream, MORE than a lot!

But there is one place, I didn't like much,
I'd get poked and prodded, needles would touch.

They ran many tests, I didn't study yet!
I must have failed, my parents upset.

But they didn't warn me, didn't teach me the answer.
I've never heard of Pancreatic Cancer.

But that won't stop me from us having fun.
We've got so many days to play in the sun.

I'm a fun, bouncy dog, this won't get me down.
"Please Mom and Dad, don't sit there and frown."

That test isn't nothing, I'll be alright.
I'm here just for you, until the final goodnight.

So let's just stay focused, on treats and a ride.
Choose to stay happy, want and decide.

Each day is a gift, worth smiling with joy.
I'm a really happy, tail-waggin' boy!

So what if I hurt, or my tummy's upset.
I'll push past discomfort, it's all a mindset.

I know you'll be with me, and that's all that matters,
Don't let the future, unknown it shatters.

For when you are sad, in my heart I will carry,
Because I'm known as ever joyful Barry.

Love to the best Birthday gift ever.
Thanks Dom

Ties That Bind

When you're born into a family,
You take what you are given,
Your future is unknown, your story's not been written.

Sometimes the best of families
Aren't yours and yours alone.
Sometimes your favorite family,
Isn't found within your home.

Many times your family, is shown to you at losses,
They're the people who are there,
When you're holding heavy crosses.

They support you how they can,
Guide you 'long the way,
Help you make it through, to see another day.

You can open up to them, and they will never judge.
Fair-weather friends, they're not,
And won't push you in the sludge.

They're the best of people, loving,
I pray you get to find,
A family you can count on, with caring ties that bind.

Written for Maureen

Tireless Tennis Balls

I never had a dog who liked to play fetch.
On top of chasing balls, he also likes to catch.
But no matter what persistence, key within his brain,
And energy forthcoming, for him will never drain.

If I'm in the kitchen, a tennis ball appears,
Within another minute, a second volunteers.
And if I keep on working, ignoring all them balls,
A fourth and fifth and yet another tennis ball, falls.

Within a few short minutes they multiply times five.
Soon I'll hear the bouncing as another ball arrives.

Then with some tenacity, the dishwasher collects,
Pay attention to the tennis ball,
The puppy doth expects.

Waggle Butt

Waggle Butt sees Wiggle Butt
Sitting in a chair,
Wishing he could move his bro,
So he could sit up there.

Wiggle Butt sees Waggle Butt
Looking at him longing.
He enjoys the knowing,
That his little brother's fawning.

Fuzzy Face sees Waggle Butt
And tries to warn away,
Knowing that King Wiggle Butt
Will always get his way.

Ruppy sees the lot of them,
And rolls his eyes around.
Why can't his younger brothers,
Calm their wiggles down?

Waggle Butt sees mommy come
And goes to plead to her,
Suddenly a growl begins,
And yelling must occur.

Wiggle Butt gets down so he,
Won't be yelled at wrongly.
Then Waggle Butt gets on the chair,
The tension builds up strongly.

Everyone begins to howl,
Wiggle Butt's the loudest.
He was in the right, he said,
He holds his head up proudest.

Waggle Butt leaps off the chair
And starts to run away,
Knowing he'll survive this bout
To prey another day.

But Ruppy is the oldest
And his barking can be heard,
"Behave yourselves," he barks at them,
He has the last word.

* *Yes, I have four large dogs and yes, that is their nicknames. Waggle Butt is the new puppy. Ruppy is the oldest. Fuzzy Face is the 'middle child' and Wiggle Butt is the special one who thinks he's a REAL Boy.*

SADNESS & GREIF
Poems

Love Never Goes Away

Love never goes away,
It changes and reforms.

It varies each and every day,
It weathers all the storms.

Strong enough to last through life,
And doesn't stop at death.

I'll carry love within my heart,
Until my own last breath.

His Rainbow

It was a childhood enchantment
That has carried to today,
A rainbow's vibrant colors,
Against a sky so grey.

The magic of that spectrum,
Has always meant so much,
Following its colors
To see if it would touch.

Hues that sing my heart song,
Against my aching soul,
Another loved one lost,
Has carved out quite a hole.

The prospect of a rainbow,
A storms' gift when it clears,
True beauty in the sky,
To wipe away my tears.

They say that it's God's promise,
A symbol proving love,
The world will still go on,
As He looks down from above.

Speeding By

The world is a turnin',
Faster it seems,
The nights go by quicker
Without any dreams.

The days blur together,
Each moment obscure,
Faster and faster
Without any cure.

I race to the land's edge,
I call to the waves,
I ask them to stop
But they are just slaves.

They do what they need to,
They'll never be caught.
They'll keep on tossin'
When I cannot.

Until the End of Rhyme

When your last night arrived, I hardly survived.
The pain in my heart, as your soul did depart.

I was so scared, as you were impaired,
Alone and afraid, that night I prayed.

Would He take you quick, lickety split?
Would you go slow, I didn't know.

I kept calling for help, I screamed with a yelp,
And yes I blame, when no one came.

Rocking my knees, begging please,
Didn't know what to do, didn't have a clue.

I watched you choke, couldn't fix the stroke,
I tried so hard, this moment has scarred.

When you finally passed, it seemed so fast,
Because I didn't know, the exact time you'd go.

You reached your hand up, it didn't let up,
And though you were gone, I held on too long.

Your passing to me, it felt like a crime,
Emotional turmoil at the end of all rhyme.

Loneliness

Surrounded by a crowd,
So much to see and do.
So many happy faces,
Like being in a zoo.

I smile looking out at them,
I greet them with a song.
Then they walk away from me.
What am I doing wrong?

No one who glances at me,
Really seems to care.
They claim they do but don't,
They're never really there.

They use me for my eagerness,
They see what they can get.
They are doing for themselves.
I wish we never met.

I'd rather be alone,
And think that they are good.
Than realize they exploit,
And use me all they could.

At least then all my loneliness,
Would not be linked with fears,
Of disappointed moments,
And fighting back the tears.

Dominoes

The dominoes are toppling,
Without a chance to say goodbye,
Cascading pieces falling,
As friends and family die.

Attempts to stack more pieces,
To extend the tiles trail...
It's going by too fast,
I'm afraid I'm gonna fail.

I really need some help
To stop the chains decline,
An obstacle to add,
To block the falling line.

A friend with an extension,
Extra dominoes in place,
Tiles all setup
To extend this life's big race.

I'm hoping it will happen,
I'm praying for that friend,
I'm waiting for that moment,
The addition or the end.

Grief

God is always there,
No matter what the cost.
He always has a plan,
So you never will get lost.

Really understanding
Is His way to help you know,
To lose a loved one's heart,
In turn will help you grow.

In case you didn't know it,
You're always in His heart,
So when you keep Him close,
You'll never be a part.

Every time you're hurting
He's hurting, too, for you,
Because He feels your pain
In everything you do.

Grief is part of living,
And dying's what we do,
To grow our faith in Him,
So He'll be close to you.

Come Home

I've been through quite a few things,
In my rather cluttered years,
So much stress and losses, more than most, I fear.

My Mother, she was murdered.
My Dad died in his sleep.
My Aunt committed suicide,
And that was rather deep.

My Grandma died while choking,
A slow yet sudden death.
And I was alone and frightened,
When Grandpa took his last breath.

I've been forced to keep on moving,
No time for grief and tears.
And all this happened quickly, within eleven years.

Sat through a murder trial, heard her call to 911.
Was told by the judge not to cry,
Until the trial was done.

I've buried my whole family, yes, it was quite small.
And now I've no blood relatives,
That I can write or call.

I've met some distant relatives,
Am trying to pull them in,
But it's just not the same,
Not the way it's always been.

Yet I will hold my head up,
Albeit, sometimes I cry.
When no one's around looking,
I look up to the sky.

I consider them my angels,
So many on my side.
Praying they'll help lead me,
Be my spiritual guide.

Yet still I know I'm lonely,
Trying to make friends,
Waiting for my calling,
When all of this stuff ends.

I'll keep moving forward,
Keep living on the roam,
Until my Lord calls me,
To finally come home.

Depression

The depression is unbearable,
The loneliness is bad,
I'm isolated, wondering
Why is life so sad?

I seem to have no real friends,
No besties and no pals,
No one can I call
No really be there gals.

I have to hide my feelings,
Pretend that all's alright,
Because no one cares about me
No one knows my plight.

My fake smile is pasted,
But if you knew my eyes,
You'd see that I am hurting,
It's really no surprise.

But the fakers do their faking,
They don't even share a post.
I'm so alone in this world
I'd be better as a ghost.

Because at least I'd know it's over,
Stop trying, no expectations.
There'd be no hope for friendship,
No need for all this patience.

Then I could just float away,
Clouds would be so nice.
All I'd have to do is leave,
Dying is my price. *

This was written during a very dark time in my life, where grief, depression and stress were overwhelming. But I worked through it, found new friends and God showed me a better way.

Don't ever take your life! Nothing is worth the ultimate end. I wrote this because it was MY way to get the feelings and emotions off of my chest and out of my head so I could move forward.

Sometimes, writing can be therapeutic. I highly encourage you to write out your thoughts, even if you choose to never share them. But if they are dire, please take those to someone who can help.

PS God is Always Listening.

BEAUTY OF THE WORLD
Poems

Rolling Thunder

Rolling thunder the waves crashing in,
A light on the crest reminds me of when,
Whispering daydreams so vivid and bright,
Within my dreams a miraculous sight.

Glittering droplets they float in the breeze,
Like moonlight shining through a forest of trees.
A castle afar, set just past my reach,
So hard to get to from this fantasy beach.

The sunshine is setting, the moon rises low,
Clouds rolling in, silver lining aglow.
Shaping the shore are the unicorns marks,
Escaping the sea with magical sparks.

The beauty of the moment, I share this display
With a man, so important on this magical day.
The spray of magic in the evening mist,
Especially for you, every day you are missed.

The Magnificent Rose

Three Glorious Roses I give to thee,
Their Dazzling Radiance Alive and Free,

Sparkling Beauty with the Warmth of their Light,
Shimmering Dew Drops in the Heat of the Night.

Magnificent Splendor, their Beauty so Wild,
Their Essence Mystic as each Petal Compiled

Their Blossoms, they Flourish an Amazing Bouquet,
Especially for you - on this Miraculous Day.

A Bird's Song

That tweet, tweet, tweet,

Is so, so neat.

That sparkling twitter

Sounds like your wings flitter

That chirp, chirping,

That marks the spring,

A baby cheep, cheep,

From an egg they peep.

And then they get bigger,

And soar in the sky.

They spread out their wings,

And set out to fly.

From high up

They let out a shriek,

So much louder than a tiny squeak.

All I know, is the sound all along,

Is what I enjoy, every bird's song.

Beautiful Views

With views like this, a fantasy-scape,
White clouds so fluffy changing shape.

With flowers blooming an artistic array,
Colors thriving throughout the day.

With tree limbs bowing, producing shade,
A canopy awning with a floral cascade.

It's a beautiful day to rest and relax,
And let all your worries slip through the cracks.

Green Ripples Shimmering

The pond was beautiful, as large as the land,
Surrounded by flowers, looking so grand.

The sound of the waters, trickling stream,
Sparkling glitter from every moonbeam.

The turtles would swim, with barely a trace
Of their presence, within this beautiful place.

But when they'd peek from below the surface,
T'was like seeing the head from a tiny Loch Ness.

Yet, in the sunshine the pond was, oh, so different,
The light bloomed algae with full intent.

And the waters, thick and somewhat dulled,
Thick-like sludge, green as an Emerald.

And when the turtles peeked out, it was glimmering,
What a beautiful sight of green ripples shimmering.

Written for Peggy

The Water of Life

A tree on a shoreline absorbed it within,
And a change it made within its skin.
It grew and prospered and never faded,
The tree grew bigger but never degraded.

As rainstorms came it drank no more.
No dirty water from the river's floor,
No nutrients within it, no coolness or calm,
Yet, it kept growing up like a sprouting palm.

Then one harsh summer turned into two,
The drought spreading wide, heat replacing dew.
Rivers dried up, lakes growing shallow,
Other trees around it turning hallow.

But this tree it prospered, it never failed,
Thanks to that water it once inhaled.
As others around it withered away,
It stood proud every burning day.

But no one ever noticed, they never saw,
This tree was the key without a flaw.
They were too consumed in their cities and towns,
Sirens and traffic and all other sounds.

Never once did they venture, to head on out,
To investigate life beyond the drought.
So they never saw the glorious green,
Branches held high for all eyes to be seen.

They never partook in the water of life,
Never drank from its spring to erase all their strife.
Never feeling the water trickle into their throat,
Where hopes and despairs would begin to float.

The tree would embrace all the thirsty and parched,
Giving valuable life to any whom had marched.
Surviving forever without needing much more,
A heavenly offer on a dried desert shore.

But they never saw it, never gave it a glance,
So they all missed out on their miracle chance.
And while they sat there dying, thirty and starved,
A world around it, the tree had carved.

For the water of life is not only a fable,
It's the spirit of God to those who are able.

Abstract Sunsets

When I gaze upon the sky, of pink and purple shades,
Mixed with glowing orange, the color all cascades,

Into a flowing palette, a rainbow in the sky,
Without a single arch, it's an abstract gone awry.

Sunsets over water, reflect a mirrored look,
That amplify the colors, my breath it almost took.

The clouds they keep on moving, an ever changing show,
Altering perspectives, as if I'd never know.

The blues, the reds, the purples,
The pinks and yellows too,
I wish that I could float in them,
And pull the magic through.

'Cause sunsets are illusions, alchemy in the sky,
Make me want to go there, take off and to them fly.

I'll watch the sun go down, colors good as it gets,
As I marvel at God's painting, in abstract sunsets.

Fields of Lavender

I want to get lost inside purple rows,
Of lavender scented floral meadows.

I want to see fields that radiate calm,
Where I can find rest, head on my palm.

A peaceful display of purple and green,
As far as the eyes can see in a dream.

It's calming effect, aromatherapy chill,
A serene display, the way with the will.

Fragrant and fresh, rising from under,
The massively large Fields of Lavender.

Crossing Bridges

I have always loved seeing bridges,
Beams are kind of bland.
But when you add the suspension and cables,
Those bridges look quite grand.

Truss bridges are neat with their structures
Especially the older designs.
Architecturally speaking - amazing,
Such artistic finds.

Arch Bridges I think are my favorites.
I love the curves and the sway.
For whatever reason I'm drawn there,
I feel like they show the way.

But bridges aren't just about travel,
Some are meant to be built.
However, be sure not to burn them,
You won't like feeling that guilt.

And then there's the Rainbow Bridges,
A symbolic beauty marquis.
The crossing of a pet loved one -
Knowing their spirit is free.

Crossing Bridges is more than a journey,
The destination is sometimes unknown.
But each step you take will advance you,
And at the end you'll have grown.

Rays of Light

Rays of light shine through the leaves,
Of trees that stand so proud to be.

Rays of light shine through the clouds,
Long lines of light look oh, so proud.

Rays of light peek in my house,
Curious brightness, illumination douse.

Rays of light, lead me on my way,
They mark the beginning of a new day.

Rays of light, like God's own might,
Reaching for me before the night.

Rays of light, Heaven's way,
A reminder and promise of a better day.

Waterfalls

A barely moving trickle, speeds up with gravity,
Water with no borders, running, oh, so free.

Ripples with a current, small stones make caps of white,
Calming sounds to listen to, what a nice delight.

The flow keeps moving faster, quicker it will go,
And it keeps rolling down the line, quickening its flow.

The torrent begins roaring, washing down the way,
And soon you'll see the cloud of mist and airborne spray.

Because the water's falling, down a large ravine,
The rushing waters white, make an awe-inspiring scene.

Sometimes there is a rainbow, a lot of times it seems,
And this makes waterfalls to me,
Feel like aspects of my dreams.

Rushing down the river, carving its name within the path,
It doesn't even care to check its aftermath.

A waterfall keeps moving, its existence will deliver,
Like all of our existence, rolling down the river.

Stars At Night

When I wake, 'cause I can't sleep,
I look outside my window,
And longingly stare at the stars,
Shining all aglow.

I think the scientific -
That they're so far away,
So many thousand light years,
For me to see their ray.

Then there is the knowledge
That their light died long ago,
And what I'm seeing is a reminder,
Of their warm and radiant glow.

And that makes me wonder,
Am I really here?
Am I just a reminder,
Am I already gone, I fear?

As my mind starts spinning,
I know I'll be alright,
'Cause they are still with me,
My reflective stars at night.

WACKY TITLES
Poems

Seeking Guardian Angel, Mine's in Therapy

I took out an ad in the paper today,
I was almost embarrassed by this,
I'm in search for a guardian angel again,
My last one is remiss.

Apparently her wings are tired,
She doesn't get enough rest,
She signed up for this job,
And she's the one who's stressed?

So I'm seeking a new Guardian Angel
Because I am unhappy.
Mine quit on me and left,
And is currently taking therapy.

Written for Linda

Toes and Jam

Andrew was a little boy
When he asked his mom for breakfast.
His mom responded with something odd,
It must have been a test.

Cause as Andrew thought about her words,
And visualized the meal,
He began to imagine the grossest things,
Upset he began to feel.

She said "Toes and Jam," but that raised a question,
Whose toes did she have in mind?
His or hers or somebody else's,
Whose toes was she gonna find?

Elephant toes would be too big,
Frog toes would be too small,
Doggy toes would just be cruel,
Without them, they would fall!

And what kind of jam would go on toes?
Strawberry or grape?
The whole thing made Andrew sick,
He planned his great escape.

So when his mom said it was ready,
To come and get his food.
Andrew found he wasn't hungry,
Definitely not in the mood.

When she asked him why he wanted to lie,
Instead he started to cry,
"Toes and jam is not what I wanted.
Please mom, don't make me try."

His Mom then laughed and ruffled his hair,
His face looked, oh, so grim.
"I said Toast and Jam, you silly boy."
And placed the plate in front of him.

Written for Andrew

McKenzie the Mermaid

McKenzie was a mermaid who lived within the sea.
She'd swim around the corral,
Her life was so carefree.

She'd play around with dolphins,
Ride whales and talk to fish.
She had no responsibility,
She could do anything she'd wish.

But McKenzie had a problem,
Didn't know what she could do.
She loved specific things,
Without them, she felt blue.

She really liked those marshmallows,
Oh how they are so squishy,
But marshmallows can't get wet,
She found that kind of fishy.

She loved to watch long movies,
It didn't matter which,
But she'd dry out while watching,
And that was a big hitch.

The other thing McKenzie liked
Was monkeys and their tails.
She thought it fun to hang from trees,
But she only had scales.

As a mermaid she looked outward,
Wishing for the sand,
But she'd never get to go,
She couldn't walk on land.

But then she met a human,
A young girl so out of place.
She was so excited
To meet a mermaid face to face.

She said I really do like swimming,
But I can't do it all day,
I really like the dolphins,
But I can't ask them to play.

I think that fish are pretty,
And corral's really cool,
But I don't get to swim all day,
I have to go to school.

Oh yes, I do like movies,
I can't watch them any time,
I have chores to do,
A curfew and bedtime.

McKenzie liked those other things,
But she realized what she had,
Being a mermaid was fun,
And this made McKenzie glad.

Written for Alysa & McKenzie

You Don't Need Super Powers To Be Super

You don't need to fly to travel,
The desire to journey is yours.
Go where you want when you want to,
A book can open the doors.

You don't need to be strong to save others,
All you need is a willingness to do.
If you can't do alone ask for help,
Together you'll all make it through.

You don't need to read minds to know,
What others are feeling inside.
Their faces expressions and posture,
Is something they cannot hide.

You don't need telekinesis to move things,
Get up and put hands on your goal.
Touch one life then another,
You've got all the control.

You don't need super hearing to listen,
When others are speaking to speak.
Sometimes you just need to hear them,
To show them they are not weak.

You don't need x-ray vision to see,
Inside of someone's heart,
Their actions speak such volumes,
It helps to set them apart.

You don't need invisibility to go hiding,
Some can't be seen while in sight.
Open your eyes to those lost souls,
When you see them, help them, you might.

Bravery isn't for heroes,
The power makes you a trooper.
See feel and hear your surroundings,
You don't need superpowers to be super!

Lickety Split an Ice Cream Fable

Rachel was an ice cream junkie,
She loved the stuff so much,
She decided there was no day,
Her stomach wouldn't touch
That frozen creamy substance,
That flavorful parfait,
So she made a recipe book,
For every single day.

Monday was always difficult,
Challenges you had to take,
So that was the perfect day,
For a slice of ice cream cake.

Tuesday was exhausting,
A day you couldn't ditch
So to brown bag it just in time,
With an ice cream Sandwich.

Wednesday was the middle,
You didn't get a vote,
and if you had to keep going,
You'd need a root beer float.

Thursday was a throwback,
It makes you want to groan,
So the perfect dish for this,
Is a two-scoop ice cream cone.

Friday was the last work day,
And she knew the perfect fit
Was a triple decker boat load
Of a massive banana split.

Saturday was for parties,
They're anything you can make,
So get creative and blend up
A fruity thick milkshake.

Sunday was too easy,
It might even sound cliché,
But this is a simple moment
For a hot chocolate nut sundae.

And then there are some special days,
And those days, I'll not lie,
Those are for something special,
A frozen, chocolate pie.

Because when it comes to ice cream,
No matter the flavor or way,
There's no reason to not eat it
Every single day!

Written for Rachel

Fences Between Friends

I lived in a neighborhood surrounded by fences,
That were built for security, privacy defenses.

You couldn't see through them, hardly see over,
You couldn't dig under, just ask my dog Rover.

It was quite hard to meet all your neighbors,
I could hear them out back, when I was outdoors.

But with no chance to see them, I couldn't engage,
It was as if my backyard was instead my cage.

They never used the front, that yard was just show,
So how, oh how, could I get to know
My mysterious neighbors, whom I'd never seen,
How could I meet them, know what I mean?

Well one day I went over and rang their bell.
When they opened the door I was hit by a smell.
The aroma was bad, and their faces annoyed,
"Why are you here?" So paranoid...

I gave them a casserole, then backed away slowly,
As my neighbors seemed odd & somewhat unholy.

They feigned a smile and a thank you as well,
And said something else that rhymed like a spell.

So after I showered, a full body cleanse -
I decided I'm glad....
I've got fences between friends.

Make a Rabbit Slap a Bear

Sometimes you say things so silly,
I wonder if it's a gaffe,
But the phrases that spill from your mouth,
Always makes me laugh.

The visuals strike me apparent
I can't help but see the act.
No matter the content or purpose,
You say it like it's a fact.

A rabbit is timid when dealing
With Critters much larger than he.
You'd never think of this happening...
Except when you set the words free.

So keep seeing saying things like your phrases,
Be proud and don't give a care.
Because if something starts to bug me
It'll make a rabbit slap a bear.

Written for Judy

165

Cosmic Toothless Space Monkeys Gumming Their Way to Happiness

Moonlight shimmers on the purple planet,
Making the trees look yellow and gold,
Raindrops filled with sugar and spice,
A beauty to behold.

It coated everything living, every vegetable and fruit,
Yet, there is a problem,
Admits the Space Monkey Institute.

According to their findings,
The substance that appeared,
Is filled with something toxic,
A major issue, they all feared.

The sugar rain effects, that would span the test of time,
Each meal the monkeys ate, was leaving an enzyme.

This plaque was eating monkey teeth,
And eventually they'd find,
They'd lose all their teeth,
A problem of a unique kind.

You see, Space Monkeys had large choppers,
Their teeth were as sharp as could be,
So whatever they decided to eat,
They'd devour into debris.

Yet, every meal they consumed,
Every side dish they completed,
Was gnawing away at their fangs,
Their teeth were being depleted.

But they couldn't wash their food,
The sugar was everywhere,
In their water, bath and soil,
In their clothes and in their hair.

Over time their teeth went missing,
All that was left was gums of pink,
But that didn't stop our cosmic space monkeys.
Of course not, whatcha think?

All they did was keep living,
Keep eating and drinking the sweets.
When you live on another planet,
You can't be choosy what ye eats.

So while it seems the toothless space monkeys
May have been in quite a mess,
All they did was gum their way,
To a sugary happiness.

Written for Angel

Don't Let Sugar Bugs Eat Your Teeth

I heard the most disturbing thing
Before I went to bed.
Apparently there's an infestation
Hidden in my head!

I don't know how to get rid of them,
Not permanently, at least.
What I heard was that there are bugs,
And my teeth are their big feast!

"Don't let sugar bugs eat your teeth",
That's what mama said,
And now, thanks to my mama,
I can't go to bed...

She said if I don't brush them,
Brush my teeth real good,
Those sugar bugs would get to them,
Eat them up, they would.

Plus, I have to use toothpaste,
Minty fresh is gross.
Why couldn't the bugs instead,
Try to eat my toes?

Those things are just as stinky,
I'd tell them, they're a treat.
And when the sugar bugs attack,
I'll stomp them with my feet.

So now when I lay my head down,
And try to close my eyes,
I can hear them start their marching,
Towards my teeth that are the prize.

I wish my mom didn't tell me this,
And I don't know why she waited,
I've already lost one set of teeth,
This makes me quite frustrated.

Written for Jo

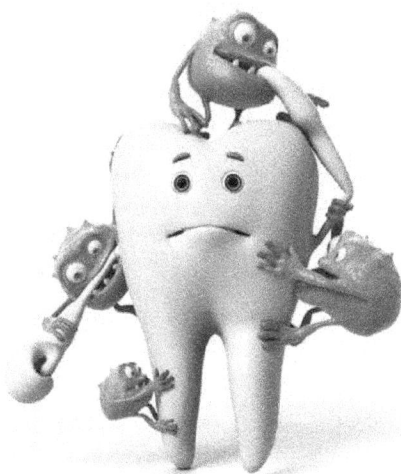

Tickle Bugs

I'd like to tell a story, about a sinister new threat,
An insect that is dreaded, the worse I've ever met.

It attacks when you aren't ready,
Won't let you catch your breath,
Relentless as it is, it'll barrage you half to death!

The onslaught causes symptoms, spasm and unease,
And many times won't stop, even when you plead.

Nothing you can do – no spray to block its path,
You'll be unaware, of the Tickle Bugs wrath.

It may sound benign, the name of this pest,
But in no time at all, you'll feel distressed
As the tickling grabs you, a hostage to tease.
As you laugh so hard, you fall to your knees,
Your body convulsing, you try to swerve.
Your skin will crawl, evoking each nerve,
As your blood pressure quickens, to stimulate,
You're laughing so hard, it's almost too late!

Don't mistake the onslaught as a harmless hug,
When it comes from the dreaded, Tickle Bug!

Written for Cheryl

Digging Half a Hole

My son said he was digging,
I asked my son what for?
He said he wanted half a hole,
Nothing less and nothing more.

I asked him how he'd stop digging,
How will you know you're at half?
He looked at me and rolled his eyes,
He even started to laugh.

He then continued his digging,
I offered to get him a drink.
How will he know he's at half a hole?
I truly didn't know what to think.

Finally he came in to take a shower,
I peered out the window to see,
He had dug himself quite a large hole,
But was his half complete?

When he came out to drink some water,
He saw inquiry on my face,
He sighed and pointed to the pile,
And explained his plan in place.

Today, I dug half a hole,
Tomorrow I'll dig the rest,
That'll make a WHOLE -
Boy, was I impressed!

Brake Lights on the Highway

You're zooming down the highway,
Keeping up with all the cars
No cares 'bout the speed limit,
Or going behind bars.

The limit's just a guideline,
Stay within 10 and then,
You'll be safe from a ticket,
When you're pulled over - again.

But in Texas our limits, 75 or more –
And if you're already driving 85,
Then put it to the floor.

And if you dare to go slower,
Or worse, before the sign,
Well, you'll be cut off and responsible
For holding up the line.

There's a section in the handbook,
A car length for every ten,
But if you try to abide by it, you will never win.

So they're tailgating and speeding,
Yeah, we're crazy, can't you tell?
But when driving on our highways,
The law of speeding, they rebel.

But then something happens,
Something horrible and dire,
A car wreck, a tanker spill,
A blow out, or fire…

Suddenly you see brake lights,
A sea of vibrant red,
You take both feet and pound them
On the brake with so much dread.

The tires they are squealing,
Your elbows locked in place,
Your eye balls are so wide,
They pop out of your face.

The car bumper that's in front of you,
Coming at you, oh, so fast,
You veer off to the shoulder,
Just in case your need to pass.

And as your car trunk lifts,
Because Fred Flintstone's feet are yours,
You start to worry you've made a mess,
You feel warmth within your drawers.

But the fear is not quite over,
Just because you're stopped,
There's another car in your mirror,
And now you know, you're blocked.

You hear their tires squealing,
Watch their bumper arrive,
You're afraid your shorts are filled with
Something that'll make you slide.

You brace again for impact,
You crunch your eye lids closed,
You're feeling vulnerable,
You're feeling so exposed.

Your heart is pounding harder,
You say a prayer in case,
And that's when it is over,
With a centimeter of space.

So you wait in that traffic jam,
The time ticks by so slow,
When it finally clears up,
You're so raring to go...

You stomp that gas pedal harder,
Flip off the guy to the side.
You race to get back to speeding,
Because
Driving
(in Texas)
Is a ride!

Boots and Spurs

Smell that leather, the texture so soft,
No matter the skin, the aroma will waft.
The color, the shape the fringe and the Concho,
When you're wearing spurs, you're the head honcho.

The band can be simple, or decorative though,
The shank is what helps to set spurs in show.
The rowel or the jingle Bobs sound out to the world,
You're heading over, don't get yer knickers unfurled.

The jingle and jang, the stride of your pace,
Just take your time, stroll into this race.

Your hat's tilted low, your clothes fitting fine,
Sure thing my friend, I'll stand behind you in line.

Doesn't matter my status, I could almost be yours,
When you're wearing tight jeans...
And those boots and spurs.

Written for Gary & Mary Sue

175

To Confusion

I know that you believe

you understand

that you think I should

but I am not sure

you realize that

what you heard

is not what I meant.

-

You don't know what you know,

but you know what you don't know.

So in other words,

you don't know what you're supposed to know,

& you do know what you're not supposed to know.

You know what I mean?

About the Author

Kathleen J. Shields is an award-winning author having won First Place Best Educational Children's Series from the Texas Association of Authors for "The Hamilton Troll Adventures".

The Hamilton Troll series is educational and inspirational, teaching young children social skills, animal characteristics and how to handle real-life situations.

While awaiting illustrations, Shields' writes chapter books for her slightly older readers (tweens and general audiences). While still infusing education into each story, Kathleen endeavors to entertain young readers, igniting a desire to read (and maybe even write) that will span a lifetime.

Shields' also runs a website and graphic design company called Kathleen's Graphics. She designs colorful, eye-catching websites, custom logos and advertisements for businesses and authors. She enjoys being challenged to learn new things.

Additionally, Kathleen writes an inspirational and educational blog regarding her endeavors as an author as well as a business woman and Christian. Her views are always light-hearted and thought-provoking and are intended to get the reader thinking.

For more information about the author, and her books, please visit: **www.KathleensBooks.com** or follow her blog at: **www.KathleenJShields.com**

Other Books by this Author

Ghost Dogs
As a toddler Jamie develops an amazing gift, the ability to see Ghost Dogs. They look just like our past pets, just a bit more transparent.

Dream World Defenders
Ryan and his friends enter the dream world where they can do anything they can imagine. The only thing they can't figure out how to do? Wake up.

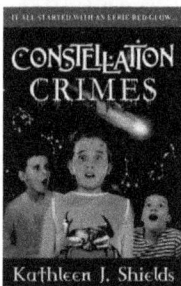

Constellation Crimes
A Giant Scorpion, a Crab Attack and a Killer Wolf – What do these have in common? The zits on Jared's face! A boys will be boys with active imaginations, story.

Ally Cat, A Tale of Survival
Allison Catsworth gets knocked off of a cliff and instead of falling to her death, she transforms into a cat and lands on all four paws!

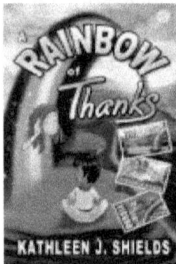

A Rainbow of Thanks
Kate walks into a rainbow and is transported to various places on the planet as she tries to get back home.

The Painting
Gerald is given a blank canvas, so he paints a world, one that he loves so much – it comes to life!
The First Book of a Trilogy

The Painting 2
Benjamin, Gerald's son, finds a way to be born into the Painting so he can tell the inhabitants about his father, the Painter.

Dandy Lion, A Legend of Love & Loss
Dandy loses a strand of hair each time he helps someone. He sews the seeds of love by doing good deeds.

The Dog Who Cried Woof
Riley takes it upon himself to announce Daddy's return home, but turns it into a game that goes horribly wrong.
Short Story eBook

Ethan's Reception
FiFi was not happy the day Ethan was brought home from the animal shelter... but Ethan was enthralled!
Short Story eBook

The Day Hell Froze Over
When the inhabitants of hell begin praying for some cold weather, the devil finds himself in a bind.
Short Story eBook

Also be sure to check out
The Hamilton Troll Adventures

2014-2015 AWARD-WINNING EDUCATIONAL SERIES

Twelve fully illustrated, rhyming educational stories for bedtime up to 2nd grade. They teach social skills, animal characteristics and even science. They also increase vocabulary by providing definitions to words. There is also a Children's Cookbook, a Coloring book and a Curriculum workbook to continue the education. Perfect for home school.

And for Young Adults:
The Kaitlyn Jones Trilogy

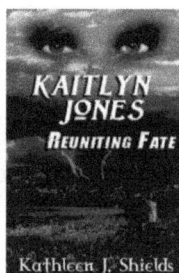

Kaitlyn discovers the gift of precognition, she's able to see things before they happen. She also discovers a telepathic bond with the guy who changed her life and the desire to help others with these gifts. Follow Kaitlyn through High School, her first job as a police officer. When she became a bodyguard, secret service and then secret agent!

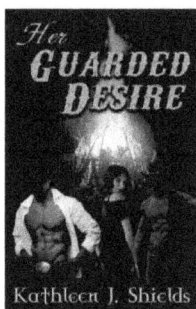

Her Guarded Desire
Kristen must decide between her boyfriend and her bodyguard, when danger reemerges and they are forced on the run.

ERIN GO BRAGH
Publishing

Erin Go Bragh Publishing publishes various genres of books for numerous authors. Their portfolio consists of a 1200 page Vietnamese to English Dictionary, Historical fiction, an award-winning children's educational series, multiple adult novels and memoires, tween adventure stories, as well as Christian Fiction. Their objective is to promote literacy and education through reading and writing.

www.ErinGoBraghPublishing.com
Canyon Lake, Texas